You Can Transform Your Life

Darity Wesley

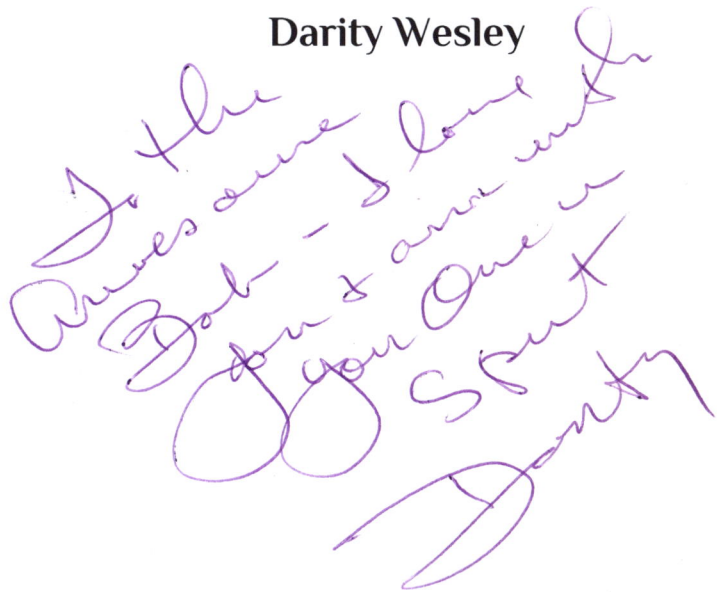

Modern Day Oracle™ Wisdom Teaching Series
Book 1

You Can Transform Your Life © 2017 Darity Wesley

Modern Day Oracle™ © 2017 Darity Wesley

Cover Design: Paula Wansley

Symbol Illustrations: Paula Wansley

All rights reserved. No part of this book may be used or reproduced in any manner whatsoever, without the express written permission of the author, except in the case of brief quotations embodied in critical articles and reviews, and credited to the author. For inquiries, please contact the author directly at Darity@DarityWesley.com.

Visit our website at www.DarityWesley.com

Wesley, Darity
   You Can Transform Your Life / Darity Wesley – 1st edition 2017

Published by Lotus Wisdom Publishing

ISBN 978-0-9995425-0-7

Lotus Wisdom
Publishing

Dedicated to our beloved
guides and angels

Also by Darity Wesley

You Can Transform Your Life ~ Go Deeper

<u>Featured Author</u>

The Word Search Oracle

21 Flavors of Fulfillment

*"Just when the caterpillar thought the world
was over, it became a butterfly!"*
~ Anonymous

PRAISE FOR DARITY WESLEY'S ORACLE MESSAGES

When I read the Oracle I get a feeling of safety, guidance and love!!! I always enjoy it and it always seems to fit what I'm *growing* through. Thank you so much for giving us this!!! - L. Monahan, La Mesa, CA

I just can't wait to receive your weekly wisdom. Darity, you really are a Star that shines bright in my life and I thank you so much.
- Stevie Rockliffe, Central Highlands of Tasmania

It's amazing how often your spiritual posts have the answers or guidance that I am needing at that moment. You always take the high road and I love that about you. You have lived this way for a long time and your knowledge is incredible. I appreciate you very much.
- Lynn Woehrle, Newman Lake, WA

Thank you for your years of wonderful advice and spiritual connection with the Universe, Darity. Your Oracles have been so valuable, and appreciated by those of us in your "ohana" all these years. I and many of my friends and family are faithful followers and appreciate your dedication in doing them. Mahalo nui loa!
- Jo Byrne, Honolulu, Hawaii

A lot has changed in my life with respect to the way I think, act, and feel. I feel your words have truly helped me redirect my path, and make me feel safer in this world. Thank you so much for your words and influence. You truly are a special being. You inspire more than you probably know. - T. Johnson

You just keep getting better and better. I really appreciate you and your consciousness. - Ed

Your Oracles are powerful and life changing. I've been working with them for 2 years now and my life is completely transformed. Thank you, Darity, for your amazing work and extraordinary guidance. The Oracles have helped me tremendously! - M. Morgan, San Diego, CA

Holy freak a moly!!! I just read the Oracle and it is OMG, it's me to a T right now!!! HUGE BIG decisions and it says "let go of fear!" Wow! Ok! - *Tiffany, El Cajon, CA*

I find your Oracles timely and thought provoking. I refer to you and your insightful topics as the 'way shower.' You are always on point. I look forward to the energy received when I read your insights. I love your Oracles! - *Linda Strom Medvitz, Lakeside, CA*

I always SO enjoy your Oracles - it's part of my daily Spiritual practice. Truly, they are some of the most authentic, inspiring and insightful pieces - simple and straight to the heart and soul. I often share them with family and friends to spread the Love. - *J.B.*

I'm at a stage in writing my book where the self-doubts are arising regularly (e.g. what the heck do you think you're doing, you have nothing new to say, your family is going to think you've completely fallen off the cliff, etc.) So the Oracle and reminders like this are a lifeline! In Love and Gratitude - *Susan Pearce, Fairhope, AL, author of OM-Less?: An Irreverent Guide to Knowing Grace*

Oh, I love receiving the Oracle!! It's as if the Oracle is totally in harmony with whatever experiences are showing up. As if the Be-ing that I AM is dancing along a few steps, pausing, receiving the Oracle, joyfully and gleefully saying YES. - *Sheila*

Each day for the last two weeks especially, the Oracle has spoken directly to me. I have had major decisions to make, many things to let go of, the list goes on. And each Oracle helps me stay grounded. I love reading them! - *Samantha*

I have been reading, enjoying and supporting my thoughts with your Oracles for many years. I find them uplifting, positive and always right-thinking. I would miss these wise words if they were not presented with such love to me each day. - *J*

I want to let know how much you have impacted my life, way of thinking, integrity, and love. Your Oracles have really opened my eyes and heart and I am addicted. - *T. Johnson*

TABLE OF CONTENTS

Foreword 1

Introduction ~ How to Use This Book 3

What is an Oracle? 5

Using Mantras 7

Creating Symbols 9

What is the *New Reality*? 11

Tools for Transformation

1. Creating a New Way of Life 14

2. Fearlessness 18

3. Trust 22

4. Cornerstone 26

5. Determination 30

6. Fired 34

7. Quiet 38

8. Strategy 42

9. The Big Picture 46

10. Uniqueness 50

11. Who You Think You Are 54

12. Vulnerabilities 58

13. Forgiveness 62

14. Gratitude 66

15. Grounding 70

16. Now 74

17. Balance 78

18. Study & Support 82

19. Surrender 86

20. The Inner Voice 90

21. Appreciation 94

22. Adventure 98

23. Fluidity 102

24. Play 106

25. Expression 110

26. Kindness 114

27. Laughter 118

28. Unconditional Love 122

29. Dignity 126

30. Healing 130

31. Illusion 134

32. Inherent Wisdom 138

33. Leap of Faith	142
34. Introspection	146
35. Abandonment	150
36. Acceptance	154
37. Caution	158
38. Perceptiveness	162
39. Change	166
40. Receptivity	170
41. Passion	174
42. Your Own Divinity	178
43. Authenticity	182
44. Boundaries	186
45. Strength	190
46. Circumspection	194
47. Life Mastery	198
48. Emergence	202
49. Connecting at the Heart Level	206
50. Confidence	210
51. Alignment	214
52. Transformation	218

Personal Transformation Journal

My Transformation Journal 223

About the Author 279
References 280
Gratitude and Appreciation 281

FOREWORD

Ever meet someone for the first time and feel like you have known them forever? That profound heart connection that transcends time and space? Darity and I had that extraordinary experience when we met years ago. We have been friends and compatriots ever since.

Over our years of friendship, we have worked together, appeared on stages around the country together and supported causes together. We even served as consecutive presidents of our local League of Women Voters. In these last two decades, Darity has revealed herself as a true master Transformer.

Every venture Darity touches has transformed for the better, even the most seemingly ordinary. She transformed the national real estate industry as a Privacy Guru when cyber security was in its infancy. Darity shares her unique talent of blending business and spiritual pursuits in the business law world. No one had ever heard of a Conscious Lawyer before Darity. She's gone on to transforming our perspectives on death as the Death Diva, speaking at conferences nationwide.

Darity walks her transformational talk. Her whole life is an inspiring journey of personal transformation. In spite of some very tough early circumstances, Darity went beyond survive all the way to thrive. She continues to transform herself as a result of a lifetime of intentional spiritual practices.

Darity continues to cultivate her connection to the Divine within. We benefit from her dedicated connection through the gift of her long-standing Oracle guidance readings. She has published them since 2006 and freely offers them to those wishing to transform themselves.

Darity's Oracle guidance gives us a compass to help navigate the waters of our ever-evolving world. These messages, treasured by her global community, shine as a north star of ongoing support to assist us in cultivating a connection with our own eternal essence.

As a Modern Day Oracle and teacher of transformation, Darity follows her Spirit in all circumstances. Her longtime motto is *Love and Trust*. Easy to say, but sometimes hard to do. As these times are changing and we emerge into The New Reality as evolving humans, we need people like Darity to show us the way. She is a lighthouse, beckoning us to the safety of deep transformation as our old ways of being crumble to dust.

Darity is giving us a lighthouse to follow to the shore of *Love and Trust*. This book lights our paths of transformation. Dare to dive in and unpack the buried treasure inside, each individual beautiful soul shining in its own light. Enjoy your transformation!

- Cristina Smith, author of *The Tao of Sudoku: Yoga for the Brain*, *The Word Search Oracle: Yoga for the Brain* with Darity Wesley, *The Word Search Sage: Yoga for the Brain* with Ingrid Coffin, and founder of the Subtle Energy Center

INTRODUCTION
HOW TO USE THIS BOOK

As this is the first book in the *Modern Day Oracle™ Wisdom Teaching Series*, I especially want to welcome you and thank you for being here as you embark on the *You Can Transform Your Life* journey. It's very exciting!

This book was designed to be a guide to help lead the way to personal and spiritual transformation over the course of 52 weeks ... a year of transformation. However, different people will resonate with different ways of using this book. I suggest you use it any way you want to! This is a personal journey.

If you choose to follow a 52 week course, then your 52 weeks begin here and now! In other words, you do not need to begin on January 1st. You do not need to begin on the first of the month or even the first day of the week – today is a good day to start. No time like the present! *You Can Transform Your Life* is structured as a weekly step-by-step path starting with *Creating a New Way of Life* and ending with *Transformation*. Each chapter integrates a new concept or practice, week-by-week, or for whatever pace you choose for yourself.

You can also use it for a message or something you need right now. How would you do that? Well, you would pick up the book, ask a question or just ask for guidance and then open the book at random, letting Spirit direct your eyes to one of the Oracle messages. Whatever page you open to, the words right there in front of you, that is your message or answer.

However you choose to use it, stay open to guidance coming from within. As you read my words, listen also for your own.

Each Oracle message and its affirmation mantra is written to stimulate both thoughts and feelings and to provide a practice to support personal and spiritual development. They are designed to inspire and provoke thought. Sometimes this takes time. Some messages need to steep for a bit.

At the end of each Oracle message are lines upon which you can make short notes, write the date and/or journal your feelings. In the lower right hand corner of each Oracle page, you will also find a blank circle. This circle is for creating your own unique symbol. (See *Creating Symbols* on page 9 for more information.)

Each Oracle message is followed by four questions of self-inquiry. The first is to explore what the message means to you here and now. The second is to create your own personal mantra for the message. I recommend you start with "I AM." (If you prefer, you can also copy or modify the mantra that is included with the Oracle message.) The third asks you to consider what practical steps you can use to integrate the message into your life. The last question is to direct your attention within. Record any messages you receive from your inner voice. Taking the time to record your experience with the messages will deepen the understanding and provide you with valuable information. It also becomes a road map of your journey that you can return to again and again. (For even deeper self-reflection, there is the **You Can Transform Your Life ~ Go Deeper** workbook.) There are also blank lined pages at the back of the book for further notes or additional journaling.

It's a fabulous time on our Planet, filled with richness and hope, and this Oracle is here to tell you that you are marvelous, unique and worthy. May your path of personal and spiritual transformation be filled with love, trust and joy! Best wishes on your journey! I'm rooting for you every step of the way! A'Ho!

WHAT IS AN ORACLE?

The readings contained in this book are called Oracle messages. What is an oracle, and where do these messages come from?

The word oracle comes from the Latin verb *ōrāre* which means *to speak* and therefore refers to the person providing the prediction or the information. In ancient times, an oracle was considered to be a wise interface between humans and the gods and were able to provide prophetic predictions like fortune tellers or psychics.

Oracalizing, as I call it, is a form of divination. Divination is from the Latin word *divinare*, which means *to foresee or gain insight into a quest or a question*. So, oracles would be consulted, in the old days, to answer questions about what to do, who to go to war with, how things would turn out, that kind of thing.

In those classical eras where oracles were revered, they were thought to be portals through which gods spoke to the people. Perhaps you have heard of the Oracle of Delphi of Greek antiquity. People flocked from near and far to ask the Oracle questions about their future, and to get prophetic advice on everything from relationships to important matters of state.

The term *oracle* has also been applied to institutions of divination in other cultures. In China, oracles were common dating back to 1600 BCE. The I Ching or *Book of Changes* was used as an oracle then and continues to be used to this day.

The Druids, in the ancient Celtic tradition, were the oracles of their time. In ancient India, within Hinduism, oracles played key roles in many of their traditional stories. Oracles still exist and are publicly accessible in India today.

Oracles in Tibetan Buddhism continue to play an important part in their religion and in their government. For Tibetans, oracles are the spirits that enter those men and women who act as a medium between the natural and spiritual realms.

If you remember *The Matrix* trilogy movies, we find an oracle there too – these movies bring the concept on into the modern world. The oracle in *The Matrix* was consulted by Neo and by others. They said she was a separate program within the matrix. Her job was to bring resolution, which indeed she did, by allowing the free will of Neo to work and to simply point him in the direction he needed to go.

Oracles are still alive and well, and they are accessible to offer insights and information. The key is knowing that oracles provide signposts and that these signposts simply provide information. It is the exercise of your very own free will as to whether or not you use and follow those signposts.

What I do, as a Modern Day Oracle, is download signposts. In essence, I just let Spirit dictate to me the words as I type them. After the message is downloaded, I edit the message to clean up any typographical errors, unfinished words, etc.

I do not feel that what I do is channeling, which is generally where a human being moves their energy out of the way and some non-physical entity or group of entities speaks through the human and brings in the message.

What I do is a form of divination. I am an interface between the material world and the spiritual world. Wisdom is offered to me, and I pass it on. It's something we all can do. The best way to get started is to listen to the still, quiet voice within, even if just for a few moments. I do it daily. Join me!

USING MANTRAS

At the end of each Oracle reading you will find a statement called a mantra. I have included these mantras for use throughout each week to integrate and amplify the energies of that particular message. The use of the mantra serves to deepen the experience of each message.

I have referred to the mantras in this book as *affirmation mantras* largely because they contain the uplifting component found in affirmations. However, there is a difference between affirmations and mantras. Affirmations were first developed in the 1970's by psychiatrists and psychologists to help people rewire negative patterns of thought toward a more desirable outcome. Mantras, on the other hand, have been used for thousands of years for spiritual and meditative purposes.

Mantras aid the individual in focusing concentration. They also help to deepen meditation and unite us with our Higher Power. Mantras are also formidable in that, much like symbols, they liberate the mind from thought patterns other than the words being spoken or concentrated on.

Integration of the transformational tools in this book will depend on many factors, one of which will be how much each individual resonates with the mantra provided with the Oracle reading. If you don't resonate with the written mantra, make up your own! Or, modify it. Let your own Spirit guide you as to what you need for that particular message. Write it down in the space provided and use it.

Using a mantra for spiritual practice is like planting a seed. The seed is the intention conveyed in the mantra and the fertile soil is the practice of it. Feed it. Nurture it. Say it over and over. Post it on your bathroom mirror, in your car or on your phone. Or find an image to convey the mantra and make that the background image on your cell phone or computer, to serve as a reminder.

No matter how you use the mantras, it is the energy which brings the seed of your intention to full blossom, to bear the fruit of what it is you are wanting. One way to think of it is that the mantra is a vehicle that helps you access higher levels of awareness.

The mantras support the transformational energies we all wish to incorporate into our lives. Develop the daily practice of repeating the mantra. This brings the focus to what you are personally working on. Repeated use supports a more balanced lifestyle. Regular use facilitates chosen changes and improves the quality of daily life. On the journey of transformation, the use of mantras makes everything easier.

CREATING SYMBOLS

Each Oracle reading presents you with an opportunity to create your own symbol for that message.

Symbols are marks or characters that represent or express things or ideas. Musical notes are symbols. The red hexagon is used as a stop symbol in some countries. The plus, minus and equal signs are mathematical symbols.

There are spiritual symbols too, like the eye that wards against the Evil Eye, which is said to protect us from those who would wish us harm. The Tree of Life symbol is associated with the cycles of life: death, birth, rebirth. The Lotus, another powerful symbol, is generally seen as a symbol for enlightenment.

Throughout these pages you will encounter a variety of different symbols. I chose to use Egyptian symbols or hieroglyphics in this book. The reason I chose them is because I am particularly drawn to Egyptian symbolism, and find them to be quite powerful. When working with symbols as a spiritual tool, I recommend choosing imagery that is meaningful to you.

Symbols provide a great function by enabling you to place an entire thought, goal or intention into a simple symbol, like a container. This relieves the thinking mind of having to hold the thought, goal or intention. This engages your unconscious or subconscious self, beyond the mind, bypassing the mind, which prevents any potentially distracting mental sabotage or limiting thought patterns from interfering. Symbols hold the pure power of the thought, idea or intention.

How do you create a symbol? You open your mind, open yourself, holding your thought, goal or intention, and let an image come in.

It does not matter what it is or what form it takes, that is your symbol for that thought, goal or intention. Then you draw it.

At the end of each Oracle message, after the Mantra, there is a blank circle. That circle is there for you to create and place a symbol for yourself to evoke the feeling, words, title or sensation of that Oracle message or practice for you.

I also suggest that you use a pen to mark the symbol on your body in a location where you can easily see it. For instance, on your hand. Then, if you want to be strong, and remind yourself to meditate or think about what you need to do to be strong, you can simply touch the symbol, look at your symbol, hold your symbol in your mind. It tends to bypass the mind and go straight to the heart.

How about trying it? Right here, right now? Make a symbol to set your intention for your use of this book. There is a circle below. Go ahead, give it a try. You don't have to be able to draw well, or have a Graphic Arts degree. This symbol is for you. You are the only one who needs to be able to see it or understand it.

WHAT IS THE *NEW REALITY*?

The *New Reality* is referred to often in this book. What is the New Reality? Quite simply, it is a shift in focus. This shift is from an external focus, which has been the way of life on this Planet for a very long time, to an internal focus that is a new way of life.

An external focus centers on *things*, whether that be money, people, material possessions, fame, fortune, status, career or whatever is wanted from the world. These are the things that humanity has been seeking for fulfillment, for happiness, for what makes us feel good. There is no fundamental internal spiritual connection, only external. As a result, this external focus makes our happiness dependent upon what is happening outside of us, out there somewhere.

The shift to the New Reality is to a life based on an internal focus. In other words, a fundamental connection with a higher power ... be it yourself, God, the Universe, angels – whatever or however you describe what that energy is. It is not necessary to believe in "God" or anything beyond yourself to understand this shift. It is about consciously allowing that creative power, whatever that is to you, to work through your life in such a way that happiness and fulfillment and what makes you feel good comes from within.

The New Reality brings with it new levels of awareness. One level is the understanding that we are all One. The ultimate reality is what is being discussed and debated and gaining acceptance in many aspects with the continued growth of Quantum Physics and the study of consciousness itself. What is being recognized is that universal consciousness is the formative essence behind all that exists within the Universe. We are all expressions of that universal consciousness ... individual, unique expressions. It is our free will which allows us to explore our true potential and express our True Selves, to transform ourselves from an external focus to an internal focus. This shift in focus is the New Reality.

New Reality consciousness is something that is growing all over the Planet at this time. More and more of us are awakening to the changes and transformations that we wish to make in our lives. We are becoming more aware that we create our own reality. Our own reality is a reflection of what we believe, think, feel and do. The more strongly we believe, think, feel and do, the more apparent it becomes that our life is a mirror of what we project.

Do we want to transform?

Do we want to experience and express our true potential, and find deep inner fulfillment in this life?

It's like the law of physics. The mirror of life will manifest what we want, but not until we decide first, within ourselves, what it is that we truly want. Once we decide, the process can start. Our new lives will begin reflecting the New Reality.

Are you in? Are you ready for transformation?

If so, let's begin ...

Tools for Transformation

1. Creating a New Way of Life

Our journey of transformation begins right here, right now. First, know deep inside that All Really Is Well.

We are living in very exciting and powerful times. This journey of transformation is about taking time to feel and experience life. Radical personal, professional and spiritual transformation is taking place all around the world. It is happening within each of us. To create the new, the old must be transformed. Some things or people may need to move on.

Take a look and see where you need to let go. What or who do you need to release? What new world would you like to build? What new you would you like to be?

For now, it is enough to just identify changes you'd like to make. Maybe even write them down and keep track of them ... adding and deleting like a "To Do" list. Let your Spirit be your guide.

If you feel discouraged, fix your attention on a beautiful image, or go outside. Look at the trees, the clouds, the plants, the flowers. Connect with nature. Feel grateful for this beautiful Planet. Find a sense of renewal.

The new changes taking place begin within. The most important process to put in place here and now, is truly contemplating what needs releasing, beginning the release and feeling the essence of what you want to manifest in creating a new life, a new You!

Let your mantra be: *I AM releasing the old so I can build the new ... And So It Is!!!*

The most important message for me from this Oracle is ...

_____

_____

_____

_____

_____

_____

_____

My own personal mantra for this Oracle is ...

_____

_____

_____

_____

_____

_____

_____

Things I can do to apply this message ...

_____
_____
_____
_____
_____
_____
_____

Words of wisdom I receive from my inner voice ...

_____
_____
_____
_____
_____
_____
_____

2. Fearlessness

On the path of transformation, transmuting fear is one of the first and most important steps. Fear limits us and holds us back. It also keeps us from following our Spirit. The journey begins with putting away as much fear as possible.

New transformational energies have been and continue to expand on this planet, taking hold of the hearts and minds of more and more people. Others continue to fight, resist and struggle to keep the status quo which perpetuates fear as a basis for life rather than love.

Fear stops transformation. Cold! There is great intensity of fear on this planet right now. We all feel it. Whatever level of intensity you are dealing with, be it personal, professional or spiritual, the practice is to stop yourself from shifting into fear! Stay strong and trust yourself. Be smart. Keep out of danger, and keep out of fear too.

The enlightened, awakened, conscious and grounded person really knows the truth of the matter. The truth of the matter is that how we respond to those who want to keep us in fear is what is important. Even neutral trumps fear. Help and support others if you can.

People are afraid, very afraid. We hear public figures and the media continually stir up fear. Fear becomes a state of being. Fear pervades everything and becomes the status quo.

Fear and courage are two sides of the same coin. Stay out of fear and keep only love. Love, love, love. Trust and courage support a fearless perspective. Maintain that perspective no matter what is going on out there!

Let your mantra be: *I AM fearlessly stepping into my greatness, one step at a time ... And So It Is!!!*

_____

_____

_____

_____

_____

_____

_____

_____

_____

_____

_____

_____

_____

_____

The most important message for me from this Oracle is ...

_____

_____

_____

_____

_____

_____

_____

My own personal mantra for this Oracle is ...

_____

_____

_____

_____

_____

_____

_____

_____

Things I can do to apply this message ...

_____

_____

_____

_____

_____

_____

_____

Words of wisdom I receive from my inner voice ...

_____

_____

_____

_____

_____

_____

_____

3. Trust

Implement and practice Trust, with a capital T. How do we do that? One way is to begin each morning with a commitment to Trust – trusting the process, Spirit, the Universe, God, your angels, others to be who they are, the synchronicity of everything.

Trust, at a spiritual level, is the integration of inner wisdom and inner strength, both of which you possess with full measure. Use it to support you each and every step of the way and through your life. It is a big step in your transformation process.

Know that everyone is being challenged in some or many ways right now. You are not alone! It is really important that you Trust whatever comes your way. So much is happening!

Do something you may have been unwilling to do. Take a path you have been unwilling to travel. It is time to trust ... your Self and those who wish to help you and be of service to you. Trust your very own Spirit, your God, your guides, your angels, all the intuitive energy that flows in, to and through you.

This energy of Trust will support you. Find that the doors to the New Reality have been flung wide open. All the opportunities, all the paths, all the roads, all the challenges that have come your way are there for your own evolution. Doors are opening to new levels of consciousness. Doors have closed to the old ways of being. The time to step forward into this New Reality is now! Are you ready? Well, ready or not, here it comes!!

The more you trust, the more you rely on the infinite wisdom within your spirit, the more able you will be to place your feet on the path that will allow you to accomplish and achieve your desires and your wildest dreams!

Let your mantra be: *I AM in alignment with Love and Trust every step of the way ... And So It Is!!!*

_____

_____

_____

_____

_____

_____

_____

_____

_____

_____

_____

_____

_____

_____

_____

The most important message for me from this Oracle is ...

_____

_____

_____

_____

_____

_____

_____

My own personal mantra for this Oracle is ...

_____

_____

_____

_____

_____

_____

_____

Things I can do to apply this message ...

_____
_____
_____
_____
_____
_____
_____

Words of wisdom I receive from my inner voice ...

_____
_____
_____
_____
_____
_____
_____
_____

4. Cornerstone

Establish a new Cornerstone! Create the needed foundation! We are now experiencing many new openings. Reality is changing. Developing transformational experiences is a practice.

Cornerstone seems like a word not used much anymore, yet it is a very important part of the foundation of a structure. It has to do with masonry, representing the starting place in the construction of a monumental building. Usually the cornerstone in a building is carved with the date and laid out with appropriate ceremony. The word also represents something essential, indispensable or basic such as, *The cornerstone of democracy is a free press.*

Establishing a new cornerstone lends us support in the rapidly changing times that we are moving into. A lot of changes have occurred, and are occurring, both internally and externally. The cornerstone, the foundation, of our transformation is what we build to support our own personal, professional and spiritual development.

We each have a mission here. This is the touchstone, from which to draw courage, strength and substance. We become more REAL and TRUE.

The foundations of our lives tend to be our core beliefs, our core philosophies, our core principles upon which we see and relate to the world. Generally speaking, these foundations are based upon what is passed on to us by our parents, our society, our culture, as well as our peers. Our perceptions are formed at an early age and rarely questioned by most people.

When we are on the path to move forward in the expansion of consciousness, where we are increasing the vibrational energy of who we are and self-development, it happens occasionally that the foundations upon which we have built our lives shift or even crash. If we are awake to pay attention, these tend to be times of great breakthroughs, cleansings and *Aha!* moments.

These are also times to establish new cornerstones, new thoughts, new ideas about who we are, how we see ourselves, and how we want to be out there in the world.

Let your mantra be: ***I AM finding the Cornerstone upon which I build as I become more REAL, more TRUE, more LOVE ... And So It Is!!!***

The most important message for me from this Oracle is ...

_____
_____
_____
_____
_____
_____
_____

My own personal mantra for this Oracle is ...

_____
_____
_____
_____
_____
_____
_____

Things I can do to apply this message ...

_____
_____
_____
_____
_____
_____
_____

Words of wisdom I receive from my inner voice ...

_____
_____
_____
_____
_____
_____
_____

5. Determination

With new cornerstones to transform our lives, let's take a look at our determination.

Determination means firmness of purpose and being resolute in decisions. This includes being determined to learn the processes and practices of transformation.

Being determined to complete goals and aspirations provides you with internal motivation and drive to accomplish whatever you need and want. It influences your level of interest and effort and provides you with the resilience and power to overcome any challenges or setbacks that may come your way. Some of the most respected and loved leaders on this Planet are sincere in their commitment to achieve their goals with integrity. They are determined.

An essential part of determination is having a goal or intention to be moving toward or an ideology to be firm about. Choose a goal for yourself, or several. Be specific about your ambitions. Make sure they excite you! Make sure there is emotion (energy in motion) behind what it is you want to commit yourself to. Be determined; get ambitious!

Share your goals more openly and with a wider group of people. Be more and more public about your determination. Being more public means whatever is appropriate for you. Share with a couple of friends who can help support you. Or, share with the whole world ... radio, TV, public speaking events, social media, the internet! Whatever suits your determination! Visualize your goals and ambitions being accomplished!

Always remember, even as determined as you may be, it is a good thing to let others support you. A very good thing!

Let your mantra be: *I firmly stand in my determination with integrity, commitment, responsibility and love for All That Is ... And So It Is!!!*

The most important message for me from this Oracle is ...

_____
_____
_____
_____
_____
_____
_____

My own personal mantra for this Oracle is ...

_____
_____
_____
_____
_____
_____
_____

Things I can do to apply this message ...

_____
_____
_____
_____
_____
_____
_____

Words of wisdom I receive from my inner voice ...

_____
_____
_____
_____
_____
_____
_____
_____

6. Fired

Is it time to fire yourself from some job, some relationship, some situation or some responsibility which is no longer bringing you satisfaction or serving the new you?

We often get caught up in something that we think we have to continue doing. It makes us a responsible person, or a person to be counted on. This can sometimes be a good thing. Other times, we get in a rut. We forget to consider whether what we are doing is out of some mistaken sense of obligation or duty.

Sometimes you need to ask yourself, "Is this really of value?" In considering whether this is true or not, take a look at whether it supports you. Does it warm your heart? Does it give rise to passion, excitement or hope, for yourself or for others? The answers from your heart's knowingness will direct your decisions.

You have outgrown something, but have been unwilling or unable to relinquish it. Pay attention. It doesn't necessarily mean you need to leave your spouse or quit your job, but then again it may. Really, only you know what dead branch needs to be cut away to strengthen your whole tree. Provide room for the new growth you are working on!

No matter what it is, your intuition, your heart, is telling you now is the time to do it. Take the risk; take the leap! Do it Now!

Let your mantra be: *I take a good look at my life situation and let my heart tell me what needs to go and then I let it go ... And So It Is!!!*

The most important message for me from this Oracle is ...

_____

_____

_____

_____

_____

_____

_____

My own personal mantra for this Oracle is ...

_____

_____

_____

_____

_____

_____

_____

_____

Things I can do to apply this message ...

_____
_____
_____
_____
_____
_____
_____

Words of wisdom I receive from my inner voice ...

_____
_____
_____
_____
_____
_____
_____
_____

7. Quiet

Get some quiet time for yourself every day. Make room, even if it is just leaving the radio off when you are in the car.

The mind is going to say, "Oh no, you do not have time for that right now! There is too much to do! Work deadlines, things to get done around the house, events coming up (whatever) and no time for hiding away! Wait till after the ... !" No, says the Oracle! No! Now is the time.

Your ears need a break! Your mind needs a rest! Noise of any kind is a distraction. Have you ever known people who have to have the television, radio, talking, something going on 24/7? This type of distraction from thinking or feeling slows down our personal growth.

It is thinking and feeling and exploring and going deeper that actually fuels our inner work, our personal, professional and spiritual development. Such work cannot be done when you are distracted by the world out there. It requires silence, quiet time and stillness.

There are definitely different styles of living. There are those with lots of action in their lives, big families, lots of coming and going, drama and just lots happening. There are those whose lives have solitude, a kind of relaxed comfortable way of living. There are lifestyles all along the continuum from one end of the spectrum to the other.

Make space for quiet time in your life. This space is where you regenerate your spirit, refresh your mind and rest your body.

Quiet time is the place where no one else is needed. You can love and support yourself. We all come out of stillness with more energy than we went in with. Meditate, walk on the beach, hike in the mountains or around the block. Journal or just sit in a room (or in your backyard on the grass) all by yourself. Take the time to honor yourself, to think, to pray, to get centered and balanced. Best of all? Your quiet time keeps you vital!

Let your mantra be: *I choose to remain vital and my quiet time supports my vitality ... And So It Is!!!*

_____

_____

_____

_____

_____

_____

_____

_____

_____

_____

_____

_____

The most important message for me from this Oracle is ...

_____

_____

_____

_____

_____

_____

_____

My own personal mantra for this Oracle is ...

_____

_____

_____

_____

_____

_____

_____

Things I can do to apply this message ...

_____
_____
_____
_____
_____
_____
_____

Words of wisdom I receive from my inner voice ...

_____
_____
_____
_____
_____
_____
_____

8. Strategy

Use strategy to ground your visions. The details matter. Let's put a strategy together.

We have been making some steps in new directions; we are getting a foothold on what this transformation process is all about. We ground our vision by putting our strategy together.

So, what is strategy? Strategy is a plan of action designed to achieve your goal. You are indeed on the right track! The time is ripe to take a look at the ways you want to bring your decisions, visions and aspirations into reality.

As we develop more self-awareness and empower ourselves to become more confident, aligned, deeper people, fulfillment comes with developing the plan. Plans are step-by-step journeys.

This book presents a plan. Add it to other practices like quiet time, journaling, continually giving thanks and anonymous acts of kindness. Practice being the change you want to see in the world. These are all strategies to achieve the goal of personal and/or spiritual transformation. Spiritual transformation causes us to redirect our lives.

Redirecting our lives is not always the easiest thing. Things may be challenging. What do we need to do or be to ground our visions? What strategies can help us redirect and succeed? Pay attention to what is happening around you. Really pay attention! Your angels and guides are constantly giving you signs, signals and messages. Keep your eyes and ears wide open!

Opportunities abound for strategic planning, grounding and how to grow. You are ready!!!

Let your mantra be: *I AM bringing forth the actions, plans and strategies that will bring my visions and dreams into reality ... And So It Is!!!*

_____

_____

_____

_____

_____

_____

_____

_____

_____

_____

_____

_____

_____

_____

_____

The most important message for me from this Oracle is ...

_____
_____
_____
_____
_____
_____
_____

My own personal mantra for this Oracle is ...

_____
_____
_____
_____
_____
_____
_____
_____

Things I can do to apply this message ...

_____
_____
_____
_____
_____
_____
_____

Words of wisdom I receive from my inner voice ...

_____
_____
_____
_____
_____
_____
_____

9. The Big Picture

Take a look at The Big Picture. Your big picture, our big picture, THE Big Picture. Rise above the fray. Plans and strategies are in place, and transformation is happening.

It is important to know and acknowledge that your Spirit, angels, guides and ascended masters from Beyond the Beyond, are right here to help every step of the way. Right here, right now; ready anytime, anywhere. Just reach out and pull it in!

Within The Big Picture you can see that your highest destiny is within reach. You are on the right path now, even if you cannot see it, or do not know where you are going. Accept that this is your state of being now, that of standing in your truth. All Really Is Well, and you are on the right path even without the end in sight. It is the energy to connect with as you look at the birthing of the New Reality which is truly The Big Picture.

Soar high above the mountains and valleys of life. Allow yourself to see The Big Picture. Allow your prayers and desires to shoot up toward the sun and release them all to the Divine. They will be answered for the highest good of all.

It is a fortunate omen when we have the opportunity to turn from duality, and our everyday lives, to really take a bit of time to focus on The Big Picture. The New Reality is the integration of Oneness slowly but surely taking root right here on our Planet. Stay aware and alert. Float into The Big Picture imagining all that is there.

Add to the collective consciousness and let it support you in new ways to engage in life.

Let your mantra be: *I remember that even when things don't go the way I expect, there is always a reason for the detour; I accept that things are happening on many different levels in my life ... And So It Is!!!*

_____
_____
_____
_____
_____
_____
_____
_____
_____
_____
_____
_____
_____
_____
_____
_____

The most important message for me from this Oracle is ...

_____
_____
_____
_____
_____
_____
_____

My own personal mantra for this Oracle is ...

_____
_____
_____
_____
_____
_____
_____

Things I can do to apply this message ...

_____
_____
_____
_____
_____
_____
_____

Words of wisdom I receive from my inner voice ...

_____
_____
_____
_____
_____
_____
_____

10. Uniqueness

Acknowledge your uniqueness. It's ok, really! We all are unique.

You are, indeed, a unique entity with your own free-flowing style of expression. Uniqueness is being one of a kind, and particularly remarkable, special, or unusual. I am sure that is You. I hope that you agree!

Your mission is to pick something unique that you recognize about yourself and see how you can expand on it. This is something you can do daily. It will support you as you step more and more into being your real True Self.

If you do not come up with anything you think is unique about you, take a few minutes to quiet your mind and ask your guides and angels for something unique to focus on. Remember, no one has the same family, goals, talents, visions or spiritual gifts as you. You are a unique expression of divinity.

Acknowledge your uniqueness. Discover that it is a wonderful experience to not necessarily be like other folks, or to conform to others' ideas of who or what you should be. It's satisfying. Bloom bigger and bigger, and more and more!

Know in your heart, too, that each relationship is a very unique connection between two unique beings. That unique connection co-creates another unique and individual form and expression.

When we understand this reality for the world, there really are no stereotypes. Each one of us is a sovereign individual being, following the flow of our own Divine energy.

Treasure your uniqueness! No one can speak your words! No one can smile your smile! No one can leave the same impact on others that you do. Embrace your uniqueness. You are wonderful!

Let your mantra be: *I acknowledge that I AM a unique entity and that my relationships are unique ... And So It Is!!!*

The most important message for me from this Oracle is ...

_____

_____

_____

_____

_____

_____

_____

My own personal mantra for this Oracle is ...

_____

_____

_____

_____

_____

_____

_____

_____

Things I can do to apply this message ...

_____
_____
_____
_____
_____
_____
_____

Words of wisdom I receive from my inner voice ...

_____
_____
_____
_____
_____
_____
_____
_____

11. Who You Think You Are

You are a unique being. Go deeper within and establish a stronger sense of who you really are. Let go of who you think you are. Get in touch with what matters most to you.

Who we think we are is generally based on what we have been taught by our parents, grandparents, teachers, siblings, friends or others. How we react to people and situations, especially when challenges arise, is the best indicator of how deeply we know ourselves, or *think* we know ourselves.

Generally, it is not until some awakening point in our lives when we begin to feel that there may be more to us than what we think. We may not like how we are reacting to life or how we feel. We begin exploring. This exploration is a useful step along the path.

Observe. How do you react to everyday human drama? What circumstances trigger you? When you become the observer of your Self in action, you discover that who you really are is the consciousness behind it all, the non-judgmental, non-attached observer. Who you think you are is your ego, your committee, your monkey mind, even your pain body. You are so much more!

Does the way you react reflect who you REALLY are or who you THINK you are?

If peace and understanding, compassion and tolerance and other such attributes are what you want to express in the world, then you will choose those attributes as your response to the human dramas and issues that present themselves to you. Why? Because that is who you really are!

How do we do that? Well, when confronted with a challenging person or situation, become one with the situation. Stop yourself from jumping in, or attacking or defending. Stop, and only then respond. It is who you really are, the conscious self, that would respond, rather than who you think you are, the ego self.

Nobody can tell you who you are. Recognizing who you really are allows you to shine forth in the world. This is part of the path of transformation. Recognize who you really are. Put into place the steps to be it. Learn how to be who you truly are. Express it all along the way.

Let your mantra be: *I AM growing and realizing more and more who I truly am and shining that Spirit out to the world ... And So It Is!!!*

The most important message for me from this Oracle is ...

_____
_____
_____
_____
_____
_____
_____

My own personal mantra for this Oracle is ...

_____
_____
_____
_____
_____
_____
_____

Things I can do to apply this message ...

_____

_____

_____

_____

_____

_____

_____

Words of wisdom I receive from my inner voice ...

_____

_____

_____

_____

_____

_____

_____

12. Vulnerabilities

One of the stepping stones along the path of transformation is allowing ourselves to be vulnerable.

Being vulnerable means *being susceptible to physical or emotional attack or harm*. When we think of it, from a spiritual perspective, the practice is more about the experience of just being open to whatever comes.

Our human conditioning has us defending ourselves every time someone says something critical, unkind or even unwarranted. We can learn, with practice, to not need to defend or explain ourselves. It does take practice. Sometimes even humor. We all take ourselves so seriously. As humans, we also tend to take everything personally. We are conditioned to have our shields up all the time.

In having our shields up all the time, we tend to think we are, and have to be, in control. What an illusion that is, eh? We have to be strong or perfect or not show our true feelings. Don't speak your mind or state your truth! The practice of allowing yourself to be vulnerable is choosing to face your fears and do it! This is a great time to explore and practice being vulnerable. See what happens!

I decided, long ago, that I was going to wear my heart on my sleeve and the world can just get over it. I am going to be me, whatever that is, whatever that means in this situation, at this time. Sometimes I'm the rock: strong and wise. Other times I'm soft, fragile and open. And at times everything in between. In allowing these opposite characteristics, we become our authentic, vulnerable selves.

This is a great practice. It will always be a practice during the course of life. That human thing again. Decide to do this now. Go ahead, give it a try. The more the true authentic self can express itself, the more love and support we invite into our lives. There is also great support from angels, guides, and Spirit. Step through the fear and become more and more vulnerable. You can do it!

Let your mantra be: *I AM releasing the façade of being strong; I acknowledge my fears and become vulnerable, inviting love and support into my life ... And So It Is!!!*

The most important message for me from this Oracle is ...

_____

_____

_____

_____

_____

_____

_____

My own personal mantra for this Oracle is ...

_____

_____

_____

_____

_____

_____

_____

_____

Things I can do to apply this message ...

_____
_____
_____
_____
_____
_____
_____

Words of wisdom I receive from my inner voice ...

_____
_____
_____
_____
_____
_____
_____
_____

13. Forgiveness

When we tap into the immense beauty and opportunities that live beneath the emotional scars that each of us carry, we free up the energy we have tied to these old feelings. The release of this energy actually frees our spirit.

As our consciousness evolves on this path of transformation, we find we are stepping more and more into our true, authentic selves. The art of forgiveness is another very important practice along the way.

Forgiveness is an important basis for spiritual work. It asserts and recognizes that we can truly know and appreciate only our own life's journey and perspective. Forgiveness comes through turning our attention inward and using the spiritual energy of love to assess relationships.

It is time to unbury and unburden ourselves from the past. This includes actions, events, grievances, criticisms, perceived insults or disrespect. Moving these boulders out of our lives frees up our spirit. This is done through forgiveness.

We all have past traumas. Some have been dealt with, some not, some only partially. We don't know what to do with that feeling of being a victim. Now is the time to bring these things up. Stop thinking about them, get them out of the mind and into the ethers. Through forgiveness they become transmuted and no longer exist. Freedom! And release.

Forgiveness is neutral. It has a way of neutralizing situations where emotions have been strong. Forgiveness does not ask us to give up our ethics or values; it is really the means through which we give up the emotional charge that keeps us upset.

We all know from personal experience that it is difficult to forgive without keeping some small corner of our hearts where we think they were wrong and we were right. Forgiveness is not just about long past events. Forgiveness is a practice to be exercised on a daily basis. Someone is always giving us the opportunity to practice!

Know that the act of forgiveness is really a spiritual initiative rather than a rational experience. It is not grounded in the emotions or intellect. It is from the Spirit. It is not the rational mind that forgives, it is the heart.

Let your mantra be: *I AM true to myself by forgiving everyone and everything that I meet, then I AM free to live in love ... And So It Is!!!*

_____

_____

_____

_____

_____

_____

_____

The most important message for me from this Oracle is ...

_____

_____

_____

_____

_____

_____

_____

My own personal mantra for this Oracle is ...

_____

_____

_____

_____

_____

_____

_____

Things I can do to apply this message ...

_____
_____
_____
_____
_____
_____
_____

Words of wisdom I receive from my inner voice ...

_____
_____
_____
_____
_____
_____
_____

14. Gratitude

Adopt the spiritual practice of gratitude! Discover being more able to connect at the heart level through unconditional love. This has the effect of moving the evolution of the soul to new and important depths of feeling. These new depths of feeling generate an energetic experience of gratitude.

So much of the time we are so consumed with what is in front of us. There is always so much to do, so much to be, so much to think about, so much to feel ... that we only move for brief periods of time to that basic stillness that represents who we truly are. Yet, as we emerge as True Ones, connected with All That Is, with our Divine guidance from the depths of our soul, we will find a place, an experience, to remind us to tap into the feeling of gratefulness for the grace of all life, for the pleasure of love and life and wholeness and peacefulness.

Becoming or allowing yourself to be grateful for what IS, brings with it amazing changes within mind, body and spirit. It is a sensation that seems to clear the mind and bring us back to the present moment, to what is.

Place your mind in the setting of a starry night. Look up into the sky, see all the stars, the planets, see the full moon with its radiance shining down on our Planet, on you. Allow yourself the feeling of connectedness with all that, the cosmos. Bring in your gratitude for those stars, that sky, the Earth, the air we breathe, the wind that blows, the rain that comes; feel gratitude for your beating heart, your friends, family, relationships and for all life forms on this planet. Acknowledge the love you feel and know that All Is Well. Know in your deepest heart that all is just what it is supposed to be. Feel grateful for it.

There is so much fear, ego, and illusion out there. Now is an important time in the evolution of human consciousness to know that the principle of gratitude, no matter what ones' circumstances are, provides one of the basic tenets of the New Reality. It is something to be cultivated as a spiritual experience and as a practice in our daily lives.

Let your mantra be: *I AM in deep gratitude for All That Is ... And So It Is!!!*

_____

_____

_____

_____

_____

_____

_____

_____

_____

_____

_____

_____

The most important message for me from this Oracle is ...

_____
_____
_____
_____
_____
_____
_____
_____

My own personal mantra for this Oracle is ...

_____
_____
_____
_____
_____
_____
_____
_____

Things I can do to apply this message ...

_____
_____
_____
_____
_____
_____
_____

Words of wisdom I receive from my inner voice ...

_____
_____
_____
_____
_____
_____
_____

15. Grounding

Grounding is a practice that connects us energetically with the Earth. It is like sending energetic roots down to Mother Earth's core and bringing back up her love and energy. Grounding keeps us balanced on the journey of transformation.

Folks ground themselves in many different ways. Gratitude is one very important grounding practice. Coming into the present moment, the Now, is another. Standing or sitting on our Mother Earth and just loving and feeling her energy is another great way to ground.

It is very important to make time to ground ourselves along the way. Being grounded means that the non-physical soul, the spirit, the consciousness is anchored to both the physical body and to the physical Earth. We are spiritual beings having physical experiences. As spiritual and physical beings, we receive energy from both of these realms, to stay balanced, centered and healthy. Therefore, grounding ourselves allows us to establish an essential foundation of balance, center and health no matter what is going on in our lives.

In grounding, open your heart to the Divine guidance which your non-physical team of angels and guides brings to you. Open your mind and integrate that guidance into your reality. Allow that grounding to support you as you create your new story, your new life, your new place within the New Reality.

Focus on your heart's knowingness. This focus will bring new information, which will be added to that which you have already established in your spiritual life. These times are about moving to a new level of consciousness. Building on what you have already done, to be where you are right here, right now, doing what you do. Know, at the heart level, that you have been brought to this exact time to ground and establish the very foundation of who you are and how you express yourself. Your inner landscape and your outer world await you.

Let your mantra be: *I have found, or am finding, the necessary time to ground myself to establish or expand that upon which I build my New Reality ... And So It Is!!!*

_____

_____

_____

_____

_____

_____

_____

_____

_____

_____

_____

The most important message for me from this Oracle is ...

_____

_____

_____

_____

_____

_____

_____

My own personal mantra for this Oracle is ...

_____

_____

_____

_____

_____

_____

_____

Things I can do to apply this message ...

_____
_____
_____
_____
_____
_____
_____

Words of wisdom I receive from my inner voice ...

_____
_____
_____
_____
_____
_____
_____

16. Now

The present moment is really all there is. This seems like a relatively new phenomenon, yet an important one on our journey of transformation.

The book *Be Here Now* by Ram Dass, published in 1971, introduced me to the concept of Now. It was through this that I learned the spiritual value of being in the present moment. I integrated that concept into my spiritual practices and continue to this day. Twenty some years later, to a new generation, Eckhart Tolle, in 1997 published *The Power of Now*, which, if you have not read it, I highly recommend.

What paying attention to the concept of Now represents is a method, a practice. It is about stepping out of the time dimension, which is an ability we all have and need to exercise more. Staying in the present breaks the old thought patterns of spending time in the past or in the future, and not paying attention to Right-Here-Right-Now. The idea is to practice this as much as possible in everyday life.

So many times we get thinking about what happened yesterday or five, ten, twenty years ago or tomorrow, or next year or five years from now. When we do that, we are cheating ourselves of being here Now ... of being in the present moment and feeling, tasting, experiencing what is happening right in front of us, no matter what it is!

Even if you are in dire straits, even if a loved one is suffering, even if you have recently lost someone, if you are suffering in any way, the relief, the balance is to take a deep breath and just be ... here ... Now.

Be in the moment – savor just that. Not what is going on out there in your life, but just that state of being. Being in the present moment creates the key that allows us to be in a permanent state of connectedness with our Divine Essence. Go ahead, give it a try right now! Be here Now. Close your eyes. Take a deep breath; ok, take another. Feel your inner body. Stay with it a few minutes, or as long as you want. Close your eyes and just BE! This practice will deepen and transform your life. It changes your perspective, helps keep you balanced and increases your vibrational frequency.

Let your mantra be: *I AM observing the rhythm of my breath; I feel the air flow in and out. I AM feeling the life energy inside my body. I AM allowing everything to be, within and without. I move deeply into the Now. I AM Here Now ... And So It Is!!!*

The most important message for me from this Oracle is ...

_____

_____

_____

_____

_____

_____

_____

_____

My own personal mantra for this Oracle is ...

_____

_____

_____

_____

_____

_____

_____

_____

Things I can do to apply this message ...

_____
_____
_____
_____
_____
_____
_____

Words of wisdom I receive from my inner voice ...

_____
_____
_____
_____
_____
_____
_____

17. Balance

Balance is an important practice as we look at what it is we wish to integrate. We are transforming ourselves from our old self into our new self. Our perspectives on the old reality shift as we look at how we want to be in the New Reality. Then we can begin to integrate and express that shift out into the world with balance and equilibrium.

Being balanced is really all about living in the moment. Allowing the future to unfold naturally from our own wisdom. Being balanced also contemplates a time of actually trusting inner wisdom or the inner heart's knowingness.

Sometimes we want others to validate us, or let us know we are doing the right thing. We already have that awareness. Validation from outside ourselves is unnecessary. Balance and awareness of it always rests within.

Know that you are in the process of filling any and all emptiness within yourself with love, compassion and blessings for all. That is a part of balance, as well as equilibrium. It is for you to do and none other!

Balance and equilibrium also encompass a distinctly non-attached perspective. Being in the world, but not *of* the world. Maintaining an equal balance between involvement in the material world and a spiritual detachment from it.

This is a time to deepen and expand internal balance. Recognize that internal balance is held in place by faith, beliefs, angels, spirit guides and even your own soul's guidance. Being balanced, establishing your equilibrium in any situation, supports you in handling life's dramas. Balance allows us to live a more expanded life in these changing times.

There is a difference between mental preoccupation with daily life and the spiritual energy evoked as we accept the guidance of the emerging light within. Trust your own instincts. Don't go too high or too low. Ride the roller coaster of life with ease. Accept the guidance from your heart. Remember, no regrets. Decision made, and so it is!

Let your mantra be: *I AM deepening and re-establishing my inner balance; I see clearly the answer, solution or guidance that I need ... And So It Is!!!*

_____

_____

_____

_____

_____

_____

_____

_____

_____

_____

The most important message for me from this Oracle is ...

_____
_____
_____
_____
_____
_____
_____

My own personal mantra for this Oracle is ...

_____
_____
_____
_____
_____
_____
_____

Things I can do to apply this message ...

_____
_____
_____
_____
_____
_____
_____

Words of wisdom I receive from my inner voice ...

_____
_____
_____
_____
_____
_____
_____
_____

18. Study & Support

Take time to get engaged in learning. Support your intentions. Acknowledge the non-physical support that is ready and available for each of us.

Learning is generally defined as *the acquisition of knowledge or skills*. Study is defined as *devoting the time and attention to acquiring knowledge or skills*. We acquire knowledge and skills by experience, by practice, from books, videos, other people, or simply by observation or discernment.

This is an important time to learn new ideas, new practices and new skills. Enroll in a class or workshop. Listen to a webcast. Research something of interest. Expand your knowledge level personally, professionally or spiritually.

Studying new subjects or new perspectives on old subjects adds to the knowledge base no matter what is being learned. It expands and enhances who we are. Learning and studying are integral parts of personal growth.

Know that you are supported in your desire and intention for expansion by God, the angels, your Spirit, your guides and the ascended masters. As we study and learn, we expand our status as multi-dimensional beings.

Part of being this expansion means understanding and realizing that you really are part of an awesome and powerful team of benevolent beings. You may have heard that you are here on this Earth at this time to be a power for change. If you have not heard that, then hear it now: *You are here on this Earth at this time to be a power for change.* For your Self. For others. For the Planet.

Those of us on the Earth at this time are here to support our Mother Earth and the dimensional shifts taking place. It is part of our own personal transformation as well as the transformation of the Planet. We are supported in return as our beloved guides and angels surround, guide and love us constantly.

Besides learning and studying, this is a great time to communicate with your angels and guides more frequently. Know that they love to hear from you. Have mental conversations with them about everything. If you listen quietly, you can hear them.

Connect more with your guides. Do some studying; learn some new things. Whatever your Spirit directs you to, listen, learn and consider with your heart.

Let your mantra be: *I AM learning and growing and staying in touch with my non-physical support system ... And So It Is!!*

_____

_____

_____

_____

_____

_____

_____

_____

The most important message for me from this Oracle is ...

_____
_____
_____
_____
_____
_____
_____

My own personal mantra for this Oracle is ...

_____
_____
_____
_____
_____
_____
_____

Things I can do to apply this message ...

_____
_____
_____
_____
_____
_____
_____

Words of wisdom I receive from my inner voice ...

_____
_____
_____
_____
_____
_____
_____
_____

19. Surrender

Now is a time of surrender. Surrender to trusting your intuition, to following your heart's direction. Surrender to putting one foot in front of the other in joy, accepting what is there to greet you at each step. Surrender old thinking patterns, old resentments, old relationships, things, people, places and beliefs that no longer serve you. Surrender to the shift from duality to Oneness. Surrender to the end and the beginning.

Surrender more now than you ever have before. There is so much support for everything you want to accomplish, every intention, every thought, every desire. As you learn and grow on the path of transformation you find guidance every step of the way. Allow yourself to surrender to it.

It is a time to feel and integrate the ways of surrender. Follow your Spirit, that inner voice, without hesitation. Surrender your pain and your suffering. Surrender what you perceive as your purpose, and reconsider what is more in line with your emerging self.

Bring the power of Divine Love to support you and your loved ones, humanity itself, your Planet, your Solar System, your Galaxy in this very dramatic and powerful transformation we are all going through. In connecting with that energy, when using and relying on that Divine Love, incorporate the results into your Real, True, Self. In this state, you will continue to see to the depths and receive the immutable truths of life which will support you in your endeavors.

Bring light and clarity to all that is going on by surrendering as much resistance as possible. Everything is changing. Pay attention to these energies. Comfort and support are coming to you from your spirit guides, totems and angels.

Let the love from deep within you well up and connect at the heart level with others as you move along your path. Surrender to the love you have buried deep within. Surrender to the love that is deeper than you!

Let your mantra be: *I AM further empowered by offering up that which is no longer who I am or who I want to be in the New Reality ... And So It Is!!!*

The most important message for me from this Oracle is ...

_____

_____

_____

_____

_____

_____

_____

My own personal mantra for this Oracle is ...

_____

_____

_____

_____

_____

_____

_____

_____

Things I can do to apply this message ...

_____
_____
_____
_____
_____
_____
_____

Words of wisdom I receive from my inner voice ...

_____
_____
_____
_____
_____
_____
_____
_____

20. The Inner Voice

As we travel the path of transformation, it is helpful to thank our guides, angels, and Higher Self for providing assistance to us with and through our inner voice.

You do have an inner voice, you know? If you are unaware of it, this is a good time to practice listening for it. The guidance coming to you is extremely valuable. These thoughts, feelings and inspiring words are given to you because you are loved so very much.

Your guides, angels, your Higher Self, that non-physical support team, is constantly sending you lots of guiding thoughts, feelings and inspiring words. Take the time to quiet the mind and listen with your heart.

It is truly a strong and resilient voice. It has been with you for a long, long time yet we get carried away with thinking, thinking, thinking so much that we kind of miss that energy that provides us with our guidance. Practice stopping the mind and listening.

This is the time. Right now. Tapping into our inner voice provides us with a level of personal growth on the spiritual path. This gives us the ability to stop asking others for their advice, to stop seeking help outside of ourselves.

We can now go to our Higher Self, to inquire within, to counsel with our intuition, our guides, our angels, our inner voice. It is time to follow our own Spirit, our own wise counsel, without any hesitation. Listen inside for your advice and direction. For what is right for you. You can trust your inner voice. Take that first step. Say, "I will trust my inner voice." Then do it.

Listen to the stillness that underlies everything. Your inner voice will guide you. Be still. Being very still is a powerful response to any situation. It is the favorite strategy of those who have real mastery in life.

Being quiet, but fully alert, is when that wisest part of you, your inner voice, will whisper for you to pause, to not be fixed or rigid with what is going on, to be like a hawk in a tree watching, waiting, expecting ... ready!

The higher realms are now ready to guide and support you more strongly than ever before. Tap in. Hear your inner voice. All you have to do is turn up the volume.

Let your mantra be: *I AM closing my eyes and listening with my heart, knowing support is there for me no matter what is going on. I say the prayer and then I trust ... And So It Is!!!*

_____

_____

_____

_____

_____

_____

_____

_____

The most important message for me from this Oracle is ...

_____

_____

_____

_____

_____

_____

_____

My own personal mantra for this Oracle is ...

_____

_____

_____

_____

_____

_____

_____

Things I can do to apply this message ...

_____
_____
_____
_____
_____
_____
_____

Words of wisdom I receive from my inner voice ...

_____
_____
_____
_____
_____
_____
_____

21. Appreciation

Consciously awaken feelings of appreciation. Appreciate Mother Earth, the sky, the birds, the flowers, the trees, the clouds, the rocks, rivers, lakes, oceans ... appreciate All That Is! Incorporate appreciation into your daily life. It is a powerful spiritual practice, and it feels great!

It is important that we differentiate between appreciation and gratitude. Although they are often used interchangeably, each of them actually carries a different vibration. Appreciation is a more active vibration; it recognizes something as having value. Whereas gratitude is more of a quality or feeling.

An example of the difference is that we feel gratitude for the food we have to eat, the jobs we have and the challenges we have overcome. We appreciate the colors, the smells, the beauty, the arrangement and the many tastes of food. We appreciate the people we love in our lives, the fulfilling work that we do, the challenges we have overcome. Can you feel or sense the subtle difference between them?

One definition of the word appreciation is *the recognition of the quality, value, significance, or magnitude of people and things.* Gratitude is defined as *the quality of thankfulness; being ready to show appreciation for and to return kindness.* Gratitude is the base from which appreciation grows and flourishes.

Bring more of the vibration of appreciation into your life. Be grateful and then appreciate. This subtle shift from gratitude to appreciation involves being more present, and more thoughtfully aware and active, when reflecting upon the reasons to appreciate someone or something.

One of the important aspects of appreciation is to express it. Everyone is making a difference on the Planet in some way. Expressing appreciation to others is a great way to be the change you want to see in the world. Take every opportunity to let others know how much you appreciate them. Be specific. It truly warms the soul and connects people at the heart level. Every human being blossoms under the sunshine of having their value, great and small, noticed and appreciated.

Let your mantra be: *I AM living and sharing the vibration of appreciation ... I especially appreciate my life ... And So It Is!!!*

_____

_____

_____

_____

_____

_____

_____

_____

_____

_____

The most important message for me from this Oracle is ...

_____
_____
_____
_____
_____
_____
_____

My own personal mantra for this Oracle is ...

_____
_____
_____
_____
_____
_____
_____

Things I can do to apply this message ...

_____
_____
_____
_____
_____
_____
_____
_____

Words of wisdom I receive from my inner voice ...

_____
_____
_____
_____
_____
_____
_____
_____

22. Adventure

Sometimes we just need to have a little adventure in our lives. It is especially important when we are in the process of growth and transformation. Why? Because it supports the changes we all go through. It lightens the tone, lifts the vibration and fills a part of our Spirit that is not otherwise filled.

The process of transforming our lives is a combination of many experiences. Life itself is an adventure. Believing that and acting on it allows us to view life in a different way. Integrate a sense of adventure into life. Invoke the fire within! Yes!!!

Where is your sense of adventure? Do you have one? Does it feel good? Is it scary? Are you having an adventure? Has it been lost somewhere along the way? If you've lost your sense of adventure, now is time to find it again. If you still have it, now is the time to expand it even more!

Life is truly full of new experiences. Every day is an opportunity to experience something new. There are people to see, places to go, things to investigate, things to learn, risks to take. Life is a spiritual adventure. Stretch out Who You Really Are and what you really do.

Sometimes we may stop enjoying the journey, or we may stop appreciating it for the adventure it is. We forget that we are actually spiritual beings. We are here for a very short time and yet we spend so much of our energy living in the past or in the future. Fully engage the NOW adventure of your life.

From birth to death, a relatively short and amazing ride, this journey of life affords us the opportunity to truly appreciate each moment. We can take more time to enjoy our heart beating and our body breathing. We can open to the unique sensation of every feeling, emotion, thought, impulse and desire that passes through our body.

How do we engage life as an adventure? We challenge ourselves. No matter what is going on out there in our outer life, we tap into our internal sense of acknowledgment that life is, indeed, a grand adventure. We recognize that everything we experience is actually quite unusual and exciting. Even the bumps and bruises along the way can be seen as unique and extraordinary, in their own way.

Summon the courage now to expand your life and go after things you want. By engaging life itself as an adventure, there is a different perspective in each and every moment.

Let your mantra be: *I AM a free spirit, not to be tied down. I AM appreciating the stimulation of new experiences, new horizons, new ideas ... a sense of new adventure has come to my life ... And So It Is!!!*

_____

_____

_____

_____

_____

_____

_____

The most important message for me from this Oracle is ...

_____
_____
_____
_____
_____
_____
_____

My own personal mantra for this Oracle is ...

_____
_____
_____
_____
_____
_____
_____
_____

Things I can do to apply this message ...

_____
_____
_____
_____
_____
_____
_____

Words of wisdom I receive from my inner voice ...

_____
_____
_____
_____
_____
_____
_____
_____

23. Fluidity

Stay fluid. Allow Divine energy to flow through. Let go and flow with the natural movement of All That Is. Different things feel natural on different days. Some are for letting go, some for being strong, some for standing in Truth. Some days are just made for not minding what happens. It seems like new stuff comes up every day as we grow and change. That transforms us and supports the birth of our New Reality.

There are many spiritual laws in the Universe. Two of them are: the Law of Attraction and the Law of Non-Attachment. Both play in the world of being fluid and allowing the natural processes to take place. Rivers come down from the mountains and run to the sea. There they are absorbed by the larger body of water and then the liquid evaporates into clouds. The clouds release the rain on the mountains and the endless cycle of fluidity continues.

Integrate the concept that infinite support is available when we allow ourselves to be fluid. Forget being rigid and striving to make it perfect. We travel farther as we let go and let flow.

Being fluid means tapping into that inner knowing where our Spirit directs: *This is the time to speak. This is the time to keep silent. This is the time for confrontation or negotiation. This is the time for resting.* As we listen and follow the guidance of Spirit, we are in the flow.

The best part about being fluid is learning to skillfully maneuver around obstacles – up, over, around – just like water streams up, over and around big boulders. No obstacle can hold you back if you are willing to surrender to the natural flow of events.

Be easy on yourself and others. Watch how smoothly you move forward.

Let your mantra be: *I AM fearless in my ability to flow freely now and to go with the current of events that come up in my life ... And So It Is!!!*

The most important message for me from this Oracle is ...

_____
_____
_____
_____
_____
_____
_____

My own personal mantra for this Oracle is ...

_____
_____
_____
_____
_____
_____
_____
_____
_____

Things I can do to apply this message ...

_____
_____
_____
_____
_____
_____
_____

Words of wisdom I receive from my inner voice ...

_____
_____
_____
_____
_____
_____
_____

24. Play

Now is a great time to let your inner kid come out and play! Are you ready to have some fun?

Our lives get so caught up in the seriousness of everything. We forget that lightening our mood, giving ourselves a break, letting our kid come out to play is important. As balanced conscious beings, even when we are in the deepest hours of grief, we can allow our kid to come out and support and help us lighten up. Even if it's just for a brief moment.

In order to get through the tough times as well as the good times, allowing our inner child to play can sometimes help. From a spiritual perspective, it is all about playing at life!

Go ahead, have some fun! Play some games, make up some stuff. Lighten up and acknowledge that at some level, the world is a playground. Shakespeare called it a stage. Play out all of your imaginings, all of your fantasies. Create playful experiences with your imagination. Happiness comes when you recreate yourself. Use your inner child to help in that creation.

Play is generally defined as engaging in activity for enjoyment and recreation rather than a serious or practical purpose. The key to down time, the key to play time, is re-creation. It gives the space to re-create yourself!

Take any pressure off yourself for now, even if just for a while. Enjoy the journey of life because the journey *is* life! Live life joyously and fully. Act spontaneously. Realize that in doing so you may cause some disruptions, yet know that doing so can bring about new awakenings.

Laugh, love, have some fun and relax. Enjoy!

Let your mantra be: *I recreate myself by recreation and having fun ... And So It Is!!!*

The most important message for me from this Oracle is ...

_____

_____

_____

_____

_____

_____

_____

My own personal mantra for this Oracle is ...

_____

_____

_____

_____

_____

_____

_____

Things I can do to apply this message ...

_____
_____
_____
_____
_____
_____
_____

Words of wisdom I receive from my inner voice ...

_____
_____
_____
_____
_____
_____
_____
_____

25. Expression

Unleash your limitations! Begin to allow yourself to express who you really are! Expression provides opportunities to have a less anxious, more expansive experience. Trust yourself to go ahead and say what you mean and mean what you say. Transform the way you express yourself.

Spirit is awakening us to so many new and different things. These times can make us feel vulnerable, or even resistant to change. When we face our fears and do it anyway, we transform ourselves and our lives. We each have unique insight and perceptions which are true gifts from Spirit.

We are so conditioned to be afraid of what others will think that we limit ourselves on a regular basis. There is great confidence that comes when you express yourself without affectation or worrying about what others will think or expect. It is time to express YOU!!! Truly! You, and all living things, are expressions of Divine Love expressing uniquely.

Be aware that your inner voice can speak out into the world. Share the feelings that grow from your unlimited spiritual reality ... your love, joy, kindness, compassion and heartfelt empathy. It is all part of who you truly are and the many gifts you have to offer to the world. Expand that unique expression and you will find it healing and rewarding.

Let your mantra be: *I AM open to finding and using my gifts of insight and perception and fearlessly sharing it with others ... And So It Is!!!*

The most important message for me from this Oracle is ...

_____

_____

_____

_____

_____

_____

_____

My own personal mantra for this Oracle is ...

_____

_____

_____

_____

_____

_____

_____

_____

Things I can do to apply this message ...

_____
_____
_____
_____
_____
_____
_____

Words of wisdom I receive from my inner voice ...

_____
_____
_____
_____
_____
_____
_____
_____

26. Kindness

One of the touchstones on the path to transformation is that of incorporating a state of kindness every day. Yes, every day!

The dictionary defines kindness as *the quality of being friendly, generous and considerate.* When we talk about kindness, we mean being consciously kind. And not just every once in a while. Kindness is needed in every dealing, every step of the way. Think about it and do it!

I was treated with kindness in the grocery store recently. Someone with a grocery cart as full as mine said to go ahead of him. I said, "Thank you so much. That is very kind." The next checkout stand opened up, and he pointed it out to me, so I moved over. He said, "We all move up!" We did thumbs up and big smiles and I said, "Yes, that's what kindness does. It's good for everyone!" and we smiled, great connection ... and went on with our lives.

Kindness is good for everyone and is needed by everyone. Whether it's letting someone go in front of you in line, or picking up something that was accidentally dropped, kindness helps smooth things out. It enriches the lives of people. It causes smiles and good feelings.

Kindness is a circular pattern. It is as important to give as to receive. Acknowledge when someone has been kind, even in the smallest way. It causes positive vibrations in all parties involved!

Kindness starts with us. As we are kind to others, it reminds them, at some level, to be kind to others too. It really is one of those contagious things.

It is also important to be kind to ourselves. Being kind to ourselves supports us in the process of being kind to others. Integrate and spread that kindness. Be kind to yourself no matter what!

Let your mantra be: *I AM kind to myself and others along my path knowing its echoes are truly endless ... And So It Is!!!*

The most important message for me from this Oracle is ...

_____
_____
_____
_____
_____
_____
_____

My own personal mantra for this Oracle is ...

_____
_____
_____
_____
_____
_____
_____

Things I can do to apply this message ...

_____
_____
_____
_____
_____
_____
_____

Words of wisdom I receive from my inner voice ...

_____
_____
_____
_____
_____
_____
_____
_____

27. Laughter

We all love to laugh. It feels so good, so light! It lightens the mood all around. A good belly laugh with tears is supposed to be one of the most healing events for the body. Find that fun factor, that giggle, that okay, this is silly, kind of moment and let it invade whatever is going on.

It has been many decades since a man named Norman Cousins wrote his book *Anatomy of an Illness: As Perceived by the Patient.* In the book he describes how laughter was the mainstay in his healing of a serious illness. He watched old comedies. He prescribed himself at least 10 minutes a day for laughter. He was cured and became an absolute advocate for laughter therapy.

Laughter is really good for us in many different ways. Physically, laughter decreases stress hormones and increases immune cells and infection-fighting antibodies. It improves our resistance to disease. It also triggers the release of endorphins, the body's natural feel-good chemicals. This is why it just feels so good to laugh. Endorphins promote an overall sense of well-being and can even temporarily relieve pain. It combats depression and increases resilience!

Make humor a priority in your life. Read a funny book, watch a comedy or listen to your favorite comedian. Laugh a little or laugh a lot. But do laugh! Certainly not *at* anyone, as we are all in relationship to each other on this Planet and laughing *at* someone demeans and reduces the self-esteem of both parties. Laughing *with* someone is always a good thing. It is contagious.

We enjoy the feeling of shared laughter ... that's what jokes and comedy are all about.

Incorporate more laughter into your life. It's good for everyone. When we learn to laugh at ourselves, our situations, or our lives, we lighten our souls.

Let your mantra be: *I AM looking at life from the perspective of joy and fun and laughing all the way ... And So It Is!!!*

The most important message for me from this Oracle is ...

_____

_____

_____

_____

_____

_____

_____

My own personal mantra for this Oracle is ...

_____

_____

_____

_____

_____

_____

_____

_____

Things I can do to apply this message ...

_____
_____
_____
_____
_____
_____
_____

Words of wisdom I receive from my inner voice ...

_____
_____
_____
_____
_____
_____
_____

28. Unconditional Love

Unconditional love is generally defined as *affection with no limits or conditions*. As we create a new way of life for ourselves by transforming our conditioning, our thought patterns, our ways of being, let's contemplate the concept of unconditional love.

Unconditional love begins with each of us. It is also a spiritual practice that can be included within our meditations and brought to our attention. The heart's inner knowingness knows all about unconditional love.

Like so many things shared in this book of transformational tools, understanding what unconditional love is and then applying it to life is a step on the path. To integrate unconditional love, we start by loving ourselves.

Who We Are is not dependent on what we do, where we were born, how much money we have, how our kids or grandkids are doing or what others think of us. Unconditional love helps us to realize that we are part of All That Is ... not separate from it. We are each part of the tapestry. Part of our One Being. Part of the Love That Is.

Feel this: Practice loving yourself without conditions. To see how you can practically put this to work, maybe start with just one issue. Think about one of the most common criticisms you have about yourself. Now, consciously transform that thought pattern. Release it. Then, substitute it with a new thought, "I love myself, unconditionally. I am okay. I am lovable."

Allow others, especially those you love deeply, to walk their own path, make their own mistakes, choose their own direction. Even if you think they would be better doing something else or going in a different direction, allow them to be who they are. That is stepping into unconditional love.

Remember, begin to put into practice having unconditional love for yourself. Be grateful for who you are. Your experiences have led you to today. Forgive yourself and love yourself unconditionally!

Let your mantra be: *I AM reaching a deeper sense of my wholeness ... And So It Is!!!*

The most important message for me from this Oracle is ...

_____

_____

_____

_____

_____

_____

_____

My own personal mantra for this Oracle is ...

_____

_____

_____

_____

_____

_____

_____

Things I can do to apply this message ...

_____
_____
_____
_____
_____
_____
_____
_____

Words of wisdom I receive from my inner voice ...

_____
_____
_____
_____
_____
_____
_____
_____

29. Dignity

From the trash truck driver to the homeless person, to the high powered executive, to the person who serves our food or coffee, every human being deserves dignity.

Many folks are unable to define the word dignity or describe what it is. People think that dignity is about respect. It is defined in the dictionary as *worthy of respect*, yet dignity is really about our inherent value and worth as human beings. We are born with it. Everyone is. Respect, on the other hand, is earned through one's actions.

Each human being is a sovereign entity, an expression of the cosmos. Really, we all have a deep, human desire to be treated as someone of value. We are conditioned by our life situations to think we are not valuable, that we are unlovable. It takes work to come back from that. Understand that each human being is a spark of Divine energy expressing itself.

It is truly transformational when we change our disdain for others to compassion. Allow and acknowledge the dignity and value of every person you meet all along the way.

No matter what roles we choose in life, we can maintain our own dignity by remembering that every person we have an interaction with deserves the same respect we appreciate ourselves.

It is the Golden Rule. Let others know that they are doing a good job, or that you like their smile, or that you recognize something in them that authentically supports their humanity. It is how we recognize God in each of us. There will always be a need for dignity and its appreciation in the world.

Let your mantra be: *I AM acknowledging the significant value of all beings, including myself, and I am treating everyone accordingly ... And So It Is!!!*

The most important message for me from this Oracle is ...

_____
_____
_____
_____
_____
_____
_____

My own personal mantra for this Oracle is ...

_____
_____
_____
_____
_____
_____
_____

Things I can do to apply this message ...

_____
_____
_____
_____
_____
_____
_____
_____

Words of wisdom I receive from my inner voice ...

_____
_____
_____
_____
_____
_____
_____
_____

30. Healing

Bring in some healing energy right now. Right where you are, holding this book, reading these words. Allow Divine Guidance to come into your life ... right here, right now. This allowance supports the opening to healing and that includes awakening the healer within.

Tap into healing energies. Open new pathways within your energy field. Divine Guidance is coming to you. Start by releasing any resistance that limits the flow of healing energy and then accept the healer that flows from within.

We often seek healing from outside of ourselves. Sometimes this is necessary. It is also important that we seek healing within, that we work with our own Higher Self, with our own healer, to move energy fields within.

Part of our spiritual growth and transformation is to realize that there is healing energy within us. Believe in your own capabilities. Believe in yourself as a healer with a God-given capacity to be of service to yourself and others in a myriad of ways!

Healing means more than just reaching out and touching someone or focusing your energy on something. Healing is a process. It is all about revitalizing Self and others! Love is the energy of healing. Pull it in and recognize your Spirit and its ability to embrace unconditional love. There is always healing when you step into the understanding of unconditional love and all of its many aspects in your life.

Allow Divine guidance to support your healing. Expand and let the healer within flow the love.

Let your mantra be: *I AM a walking meditation connecting with the Divine. I meditate upon my own healing energy and my ability to apply it along the way ... And So It Is!!!*

The most important message for me from this Oracle is ...

_____

_____

_____

_____

_____

_____

_____

My own personal mantra for this Oracle is ...

_____

_____

_____

_____

_____

_____

_____

Things I can do to apply this message ...

_____

_____

_____

_____

_____

_____

_____

Words of wisdom I receive from my inner voice ...

_____

_____

_____

_____

_____

_____

_____

31. Illusion

It's time to break our attachment to that illusion out there!

It is true what they say, *it is all an illusion*. Part of transforming ourselves is the awakening process that naturally occurs. It is time to wake up! Time to awaken from our false perception of reality and become a more conscious being. Awakening is a very real part of our transformation.

We have the opportunity at this time to very clearly see the illusion and to pierce the veil to see deeper into what this life really is ... what reality *really* is. The consciousness of it all, the mystical path, is available to us as we move beyond this illusion, this delusion.

Realize it is all a mind game of interpretation and perspective. The ego is invested in illusion. The Spirit moves us to a new level of imagining and visioning with more and more power.

Energies change and they are changing in a big way. You have many opportunities to be Who You Really Are at this time. Step out of the illusion and into the New Reality. In the New Reality, illumination is key. Open yourself to guides, angels, Spirit, God ... the Universe.

If this concept of illusion is new to you, it would be good to spend some time with this. Meditate on it, pray about it. Information will come if you open yourself to the idea and ask the Universe, Mission Control, your guides and angels, God, Source, whatever that is for you, to support you in stepping up to a new level of understanding and breaking through it.

Don't get caught up in the endless machinations of the mind. Dive deep, deep in the abyss, the unknown, the universal unconscious. Regain your true nature to move beyond the stasis of the illusion. Re-emerge and rebirth your True Self to this new world.

Let your mantra be: *I AM watching for false expectations and for seeing only what I want to see. I AM opening my eyes to a new vision of All That Is ... And So It Is!!!*

_____

_____

_____

_____

_____

_____

_____

_____

_____

_____

_____

_____

_____

_____

The most important message for me from this Oracle is ...

_____

_____

_____

_____

_____

_____

_____

My own personal mantra for this Oracle is ...

_____

_____

_____

_____

_____

_____

_____

_____

Things I can do to apply this message ...

_____
_____
_____
_____
_____
_____
_____

Words of wisdom I receive from my inner voice ...

_____
_____
_____
_____
_____
_____
_____

32. Inherent Wisdom

Tap into your inherent wisdom. We all have it. Not everyone knows it or recognizes it but it's an integral part of being human.

Inherent wisdom, or original wisdom, relates to that level of knowledge that comes from the universal collective unconscious. Each and every soul or spirit is within that collective. It is within each of us. It is *within* you, not external to you. It is not something you learn, it is something you have, something you know at the deepest level.

Tap into this level of knowledge within yourself at any time. Find its source, which is part of the ability to function from the heart center as opposed to always from the mind. Express it out to the world. Use it in your meditations or prayers. Dropping from the mind into the heart is a spiritual practice worth stepping into. It brings peace and balance into life.

Inherent wisdom also brings with it a calm, reflective, stoic sense of self and a knowingness of the truth in any situation. Some call it a *BS meter*. It really is. Humans know if someone is telling the truth or not. We feel it. Not everyone acknowledges it, but it is definitely true. The transparency of the energies in today's changing world make it much more available than ever before. Open your eyes, ears and heart and you will know. Intuit the truth of the matter.

Part of accessing and acknowledging this truth, this inherent wisdom, is understanding that you have the ability to see to the bottom of things. You can listen and sound out the truth. No need to be blown about by others telling you *the way it is* or *what this reality all means*. Sink an anchor into your own heart. Bring forth your own inherent wisdom. Anytime. Anywhere. It is there waiting for you, deep within.

Let your mantra be: *I AM calm and reflective as I allow my inherent wisdom to guide my way, step-by-step, through every life situation ... And So It Is!!!*

The most important message for me from this Oracle is ...

_____

_____

_____

_____

_____

_____

_____

My own personal mantra for this Oracle is ...

_____

_____

_____

_____

_____

_____

_____

Things I can do to apply this message ...

_____

_____

_____

_____

_____

_____

_____

Words of wisdom I receive from my inner voice ...

_____

_____

_____

_____

_____

_____

_____

_____

33. Leap of Faith

Sometimes you just have to take a leap of faith. Is it time for you to do that? Have you been thinking of something you want to do and holding yourself back? Is there something you want to say or be but have been afraid, unsure or limiting yourself? Now is a great time to take that leap of faith! Face the fear and do it anyway!

There are so many positive feelings that come from facing our fears. It really gets us to the next level of whatever we are wanting. It feels so good.

Take that step. The support you need will come. The step does not have to be something external. It can be a commitment to do something for yourself, to begin a particular spiritual practice, to begin being more real in some situation or to give up pretending and just say it the way it is. What is your leap of faith?

Sometimes it takes some guts ... that leap of faith. To suit up and stand up and be real! Oh yes! We are on the path of changing ourselves, altering the way we see things, growing up in many ways. We step out and take that leap of faith. It becomes our practice, whenever we find ourselves facing a fear. Hard? Yes, sometimes. Sometimes not. Sometimes taking the leap of faith changes everything!

Make the changes you may have been pondering. Trust in your heart's knowingness. It is your very own truth, your very own heart, that tells you that truth. It is your very own responsibility to listen to that truth within yourself.

Leaps of faith involve trusting God, the Universe, Spirit, Love, All That Is ... whatever you call that energy. It is not about hoping that it will turn out. It is about knowing it is ok and the right thing to do. This is a very exciting time. Connect with your angels, guides and Spirit – listen with your heart ... and take that leap!

Let your mantra be: *I AM taking a leap of faith, trusting God, my angels, my non-physical support team in taking that step, knowing All Really Is Well ... And So It Is!!!*

The most important message for me from this Oracle is ...

_____

_____

_____

_____

_____

_____

_____

My own personal mantra for this Oracle is ...

_____

_____

_____

_____

_____

_____

_____

Things I can do to apply this message ...

_____
_____
_____
_____
_____
_____
_____

Words of wisdom I receive from my inner voice ...

_____
_____
_____
_____
_____
_____
_____

34. Introspection

Introspection is the act of looking within. How do we think? How do we feel? How do we form concepts, ideas and judgments? How do we analyze our values, feelings and relationships? Look within in a deep and non-judgmental manner.

Introspection plays a large part in the way people form their self-identity. Much of this self-identity, this sense of personal self, has been conditioned from an early age by parents, grandparents, siblings, teachers, friends and a wide variety of other outside influences.

As we shift and transform to become our authentic selves, we have to go within, introspect, to check out whether the values, beliefs and attitudes, the conditioning we have received, still holds true for us. Do they still work? Do they still mean the same thing? Some yes, some no. Go inward. Upgrade to what YOU truly and currently believe.

Introspection also can provide a form of meditative connection to the stillness that lies beneath everything. Allow things to float to the surface. It is hard to confront those more difficult areas that we hide within ourselves, our shadow side. Allow yourself the time and space to make some evaluations about your very own self-identity.

Observe how individual personality traits impact how you think about your Self and others. This process of introspection can lead to more self-knowledge. Change the behavior or character traits you would like to change. Express the real you. Go ahead. Take a look inside today. Do it consciously and lovingly. Be kind to yourself ... very, very, very kind.

Let your mantra be: *I AM going within to raise my vibration and energies to become more and more authentically who I truly am ... And So It Is!!!*

The most important message for me from this Oracle is ...

_____
_____
_____
_____
_____
_____
_____

My own personal mantra for this Oracle is ...

_____
_____
_____
_____
_____
_____
_____

Things I can do to apply this message ...

_____

_____

_____

_____

_____

_____

_____

Words of wisdom I receive from my inner voice ...

_____

_____

_____

_____

_____

_____

_____

35. Abandonment

What can abandonment be about as an Oracle message on the path of transformation? It seems pretty odd, don't you think?

Abandonment is generally defined as *the act of ceasing to support or look after someone or something.* The energy of abandonment, that ceasing to support or look after someone or something, is a useful practice at various times in our lives. Especially when we are working on personal development issues. Why? Because there truly are times when we have done all we can. It becomes totally necessary for us to recognize that the situation, issue, drama or person is causing us so much internal grief, time and energy that it must simply be abandoned and let go. Whatever it is cannot or will not be resolved or changed. It is time to say, "Enough!"

End a situation, issue, drama, or put a person out of your life, for your own well-being. Do it consciously. Choose. Consciously let it go. While sometimes it is difficult to handle the feelings that come with the decision to abandon something, often it is the beginning of a change that is necessary to bring something new and fresh into your life. Sometimes it is a turning point that will bring new situations, friends and experiences. Do not allow fear to stop you from abandoning what needs to be abandoned.

Spiritually, the concept of abandonment can be characterized as one of sacrifice. Remember that the old self must be left behind before spiritual rebirth can take place. It is not only personal, but planetary. There is so much going on with that, eh? Just take notice as you pay attention along the way that you may be called upon to leave something behind. It's ok ... let it go.

Let your mantra be: *I let go and fall to the bottom ... I do not resist ... I slip and slide and from there regenerate and create new conditions for my life ... And So It Is!!!*

The most important message for me from this Oracle is ...

_____

_____

_____

_____

_____

_____

_____

My own personal mantra for this Oracle is ...

_____

_____

_____

_____

_____

_____

_____

Things I can do to apply this message ...

_____
_____
_____
_____
_____
_____
_____

Words of wisdom I receive from my inner voice ...

_____
_____
_____
_____
_____
_____
_____

36. Acceptance

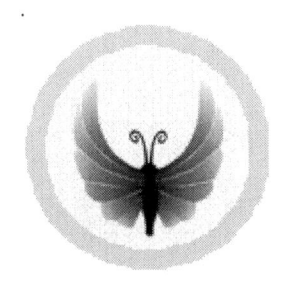

Acceptance supports our mental, physical and spiritual well-being. The opposite of acceptance is resistance to what is going on. This resistance or interference tends to cause us internal stress. Acceptance of what is happening in front of you is a way to relieve that internal stress, every time.

The dictionary definition of acceptance is *an action of consenting to receive or undertaking something offered.* Psychologically, acceptance refers to *a person's approval of the reality of the situation.* It is about recognizing a condition without attempting to change it. To not resist, to accept what is happening, is acknowledging that whatever is going on in your life is there for your experience. This is a spiritual practice that becomes stronger the more it becomes a habit.

This practice of acceptance does not mean in any way that we are to accept others' mistreatment of us or allow ourselves to be bullied or berated. The first step, taking definitive steps for our own well-being, is to acknowledge and accept that this is here for our experience. Don't like it? Change it up.

Part of mastering life includes exercising the concept of accepting everything. Very much easier to say than to do. It is a practice, something to integrate and work on along the way.

This acceptance concept really comes from the most ancient of times. Back then it was expressed that we must learn to accept everything that fate brings us. It was lost somewhere along the way. The ancients also knew our worth is not determined by external circumstances but by the degree with which we manifest and express our Divine Essence, our Spirit, God, All That Is. It is about learning to be content in any and all conditions. Whether people vilify or glorify us, neither must change our inner attitude.

Let your mantra be: *I trust my Spirit's directions as I exercise the practice of acceptance all along the way ... And So It Is!!!*

The most important message for me from this Oracle is ...

_____

_____

_____

_____

_____

_____

_____

My own personal mantra for this Oracle is ...

_____

_____

_____

_____

_____

_____

_____

_____

Things I can do to apply this message ...

_____
_____
_____
_____
_____
_____
_____

Words of wisdom I receive from my inner voice ...

_____
_____
_____
_____
_____
_____
_____

37. Caution

Sometimes on the path of transformation, there are times to be cautious. We are out and about in the world, handling the comings and goings in our lives. The practice of exercising caution is not to be a fearful exercise. Know in your heart of hearts that All Is Well; keep your heart and eyes open. Be discerning.

The word caution and the energies to explore it indicate that we are to take care to avoid danger, mistakes or obstacles that may pop up along the way. Stay aware and alert. Pay attention. Keep your eyes wide open. Keep an eye on everything coming in.

It does not necessarily portend anything untoward happening. It is a signpost for really working on being present. Not getting too far off course into the illusion, or into fantasies, or into listening to what is going on in the mind. Be Here Now. Pay attention to what is happening. Adjust or negotiate as necessary. Watch for details or issues that should, could or would be addressed.

This signpost also points to a practice of exercising caution in drawing conclusions, to be careful when making judgments or assumptions. Superficial appearances or other manifestations of what may be perceived as reality can lead us astray without further research, review and reconsideration. Don't jump to conclusions too quickly. The world of illusion has many facades.

Remind yourself constantly to Be Here Now. Bring yourself back to the present moment. All day and every day.

Every time you find yourself off on some mental journey, some jaunt that has nothing to do with what is going on in front of you, bring yourself back and stay tuned in to present time. Watch with care what you are doing. Be cautious mentally, physically and spiritually in the sense of being watchful. Like the hawk in the tree. Use your keen powers of observation to intuit any situation.

Let your mantra be: *I AM cautious with where I am going, what I am doing, what others are doing, knowing All Is Well as I stay aware and alert along the path ... And So It Is!!!*

The most important message for me from this Oracle is ...

_____

_____

_____

_____

_____

_____

_____

My own personal mantra for this Oracle is ...

_____

_____

_____

_____

_____

_____

_____

_____

Things I can do to apply this message ...

_____

_____

_____

_____

_____

_____

_____

Words of wisdom I receive from my inner voice ...

_____

_____

_____

_____

_____

_____

_____

38. Perceptiveness

Part of our personal and spiritual transformation experience is to heighten the intensity of our perceptions. Paying more attention to spiritual practices instead of who did what to whom is a change many folks never get to.

As we open and expand our intuition through spiritual practice, we can really feel what others are saying, thinking or feeling. We can intuit whether they are speaking the truth, making up stuff or omitting things. We can also tell whether they are truly expressing how they feel. It is almost like being psychic, right? This ability has always been part of the human psyche and now, with the amazing and powerful changes happening on this Planet, it is becoming more obvious.

Our perceptions about truth and authenticity are really needed now to discern what is really going on. The density of the third dimension, duality, is breaking up more and more. We become more conscious of the fifth dimension and the New Reality of Unity Consciousness, Oneness.

As we integrate and grow in consciousness, our ability to perceive needs to broaden even more. It needs to become wider, broader, deeper. We need to have peripheral vision of perception.

We've all walked with blinders on through this reality. We think this illusion is real and believe it to be true. We are being given the opportunity to drop those blinders, or at least open them up some! We can understand much more of what is going on at many levels when we choose to release those blinders. We will be able to pick something up and discern, is this real? Is it right, true for me? Or is it something to let pass? Something that is meant for someone else's discernment or perception?

The need to perceive – to see – deep and wide – is very important to our spiritual development and that of our Planet. It doesn't matter if we share our perceptions with anyone or not. What's important is that we meditate on them and contemplate how we can use this wonderful gift of sight to grow and change.

Let your mantra be: *I AM living in the light of more conscious perceptions in my world without any fear ... And So It Is!!!*

The most important message for me from this Oracle is ...

_____
_____
_____
_____
_____
_____
_____

My own personal mantra for this Oracle is ...

_____
_____
_____
_____
_____
_____
_____

Things I can do to apply this message ...

_____

_____

_____

_____

_____

_____

_____

Words of wisdom I receive from my inner voice ...

_____

_____

_____

_____

_____

_____

_____

_____

39. Change

Significant and very real and rapid change is happening on this Planet. Everyone is experiencing these feelings at some level. It is not just that we are experiencing these feelings ... change is upon us. Integrate the feelings and experiences that change brings. This integration supports the renovation of our lives.

Our attitude toward change makes a difference. Embrace? Resist? Incorporate? Run screaming in the other direction? Nothing ever really remains the same. Integrating the broad consciousness that change is the only constant supports our personal growth and ability to deal with changes.

The dictionary definition of change is *to make the form, nature, content, future course of something different from what it is or from what it would be if left alone.* There is certainly planned change, changes we decide we want to make. Even those planned changes tend to cause emotional and psychological impacts we have to deal with.

It seems that humans instinctively want to avoid change. It is very safe to be in our comfort zones where everything is known, with no shake-ups, disturbances or interruptions to our schedules or lives. However, there is not much personal or spiritual growth with staying safe, staying put or hiding away.

If we let it, change awakens us to the sacred process that it is. Change allows us to shift our consciousness. It continually offers personal insight and opportunity for growth. It challenges us to accept that which lies in front of us without resistance. Ultimately it can bring us closer to God, Spirit, angels, guides and non-physical connections and provide a significant opportunity for conscious expansion.

Here is an opportunity to change thoughts and feelings about change. Change, when lived as a spiritual process, provides the opportunity for spiritual transformation.

Let your mantra be: ***I AM paying attention to and honoring all the changes in my life ... And So It Is!!!***

The most important message for me from this Oracle is ...

_____

_____

_____

_____

_____

_____

_____

My own personal mantra for this Oracle is ...

_____

_____

_____

_____

_____

_____

_____

Things I can do to apply this message ...

_____
_____
_____
_____
_____
_____
_____
_____

Words of wisdom I receive from my inner voice ...

_____
_____
_____
_____
_____
_____
_____
_____

40. Receptivity

Stay open and receptive to Spirit's guidance as you walk your path. There is much information coming in to you. Stay aware and alert. Listen with your heart.

Know that receptivity is working when we are receptive and open to everything that is high and beautiful. We are receptive to the high road, to doing the right thing. We allow Spirit, God, the Universe, our angels, our guides, whatever that is for us, to work through us. We are willing to and willingly follow the will of our Spirit.

Spiritual receptivity involves a deeper understanding. It is a universal aspect that keeps us and the world around us in balance. It supports us with all the people and all the situations we are connected to. It is our reliance on things beyond the realm of the visible. It inspires us. If we are spiritually receptive, we do not need to be in charge of everyone and everything. Or anyone, or anything. We can relinquish the illusion of control by moving our thoughts differently. We look at life and events as having special meaning.

When we are open, spiritually receptive, we are less likely to be tempted to become impressionable. Impressionable to what others say or do or tell us to say or do or tell us what is best for us to say or do. That is not the highest use of this energy. That would mean that we were allowing others to unduly influence us. In other words, not standing in our own truth.

It is each of us, standing in our own truth, that knows. It is you, standing in your truth, standing in the truth of Who You Are, that knows what you want to say or do!

So we become more reverent, more appreciative as we embody and embrace receptivity. We choose to see through the illusion of separation and move more and more into understanding Oneness. *How* we are being receptive is as important an analysis as making sure we *are* receptive.

Let your mantra be: *I observe the forces at play around me and am receptive as my Spirit, guides and angels direct me to a deeper level of understanding ... And So It Is!!!*

The most important message for me from this Oracle is ...

My own personal mantra for this Oracle is ...

Things I can do to apply this message ...

_____
_____
_____
_____
_____
_____
_____

Words of wisdom I receive from my inner voice ...

_____
_____
_____
_____
_____
_____
_____

41. Passion

Tapping into our passionate expression is a powerful tool in changing our lives. There is often a misunderstanding about passion as most equate it to romance. While it certainly is defined as *strong emotion*, sometimes barely under control, it is definitely not just aligned with romantic pursuits. Tapping into or finding our passion is another one of those signposts that support our stepping into learning to be more our True Selves than who we were conditioned to be.

Your fortune lies where your passion is. Passionate living is one of the keys to living a healthy, happy, fulfilled life. How do we do that? How do we find our passion?

Pay attention to what inspires you and what stirs your emotions. Find your passion where you discover what really turns you on. We all know that life is short. The best time to change is now! Put some energy into exploring what makes you come alive. It is powerful. Don't worry about what the world needs. Find what makes *you* come alive and do that. The world needs more people functioning and feeling fully alive.

There are many ways to find your passion. There are quizzes. There are articles. There are books. It does not matter what you use so long as the journey is begun. If we lose track of time doing something – we are engaged. That's a clue! Remembering what we loved to do as a kid can lead the way. Inventorying talents may provide a window into where we can change what we are doing, where we are going, who we are going with.

It is really all about following the beat of your heart. In order to tap into your passion, abandon your reservations, be vulnerable, don't think about it, add some spontaneity to it all. Take the risk and allow your passions to come to the top. Act! Live! Love! Enjoy! Who cares what others think? Have the courage to be your passionate self!!! Step into it!

Let your mantra be: *I AM thrilled and excited to step into my passionate self ... And So It Is!!!*

The most important message for me from this Oracle is ...

My own personal mantra for this Oracle is ...

Things I can do to apply this message ...

_____
_____
_____
_____
_____
_____
_____

Words of wisdom I receive from my inner voice ...

_____
_____
_____
_____
_____
_____
_____
_____

42. Your Inner Divinity

Realize and celebrate your spiritual growth! Rejoice in the many gifts received along the way! Revel in your progress!

Part of the expansion of our spiritual consciousness is coming to a realization about our understanding of God. The shift that has happened on this Planet has revised and expanded our relationship with Divinity. On the spiritual path some have come to open to the fact that God is not some man up in the sky with a human personality. We have all heard that we are *created in the image of God.* This led to the perception that God is like a human. It is actually the other way around. We are a spark of that Divine Energy, an expression of the Divine. We are multi-dimensional, divine beings and are a piece of that love in physical form.

We are in a dense realm of duality. We are coming to understand Oneness. That we, the Planet, the sky, the rocks, the trees, the Solar System, the Galaxy, the Cosmos are all that same love, that same energy expressed in a different way. We are learning what love really is and how it acts. We are aligning our actions, thoughts and beliefs to support that love on this Planet. This is our inner Divinity.

At this time, in the stillness of meditation, be with your own Divinity. Connect with your Divine Essence. Pause and quietly rejoice in the feeling of Oneness with the Universe. At some point in life we became aware that there is more to life that just what we perceive with our physical senses alone. At that moment our spirituality was born.

It is within spirituality that the New Reality is being created, and that the New Landscape is appearing. The new, true you becomes a reality. It is your spirituality which gets you up and through whatever it is you create or co-create with others. It is, indeed, your foundation! Celebrate it!!!

Let your mantra be: *I celebrate the birth and expansion of my spirituality ... And So It Is!!!*

The most important message for me from this Oracle is ...

_____

_____

_____

_____

_____

_____

_____

My own personal mantra for this Oracle is ...

_____

_____

_____

_____

_____

_____

_____

_____

Things I can do to apply this message ...

_____

_____

_____

_____

_____

_____

_____

Words of wisdom I receive from my inner voice ...

_____

_____

_____

_____

_____

_____

_____

43. Authenticity

With personal as well as spiritual growth comes the realization that being our True Self, breaking free from the limitations and conditionings of the past and moving to a more passionate level of living, creates a more authentic person.

Being more authentic means learning to drop all the pretenses and affectations. It is time to overcome what we have been taught is proper, to rise above our conditioning or our mind's crazy machinations when something happens to or for us. It is time to move more and more into expressing that true authentic self. It's about upping the ante and not pretending anymore.

So, authenticity, what does it mean? The dictionary defines authenticity as *the quality of being authentic* and defines authentic as *real or genuine, true and accurate*. It comes from a Greek word meaning *to master* and before that a Sanskrit word meaning *he gains*. It would seem then that the general meaning, for our purposes here, is being real and genuine, true and accurate, being true to yourself and who you are.

Drop the pretentions, protections and affectations. Allow yourself to be vulnerable and step out with your real self hanging out.

This process of being authentic has a twofold experience: fear and then confidence. First, fear, especially in the beginning, because we are frightened of what someone might think or say. They might think bad of us, or not like us, or make fun of us, or make us feel diminished somehow if we state our truth without any compunction. Second comes confidence and satisfaction, because when we grow up, when we truly become mentally and spiritually healthy, we know that we are not in the world to live up to anyone else's expectations. When we are mentally healthy we know that there will be people who like us and those who do not like us. We really don't need to try to be anything other than our real selves.

Step into your real True Self. Be wholly who you are. Do your best, and love yourself for it.

Let your mantra be: *I AM stepping into being real, no matter what ... exploring and expressing who I am in each and every moment ... And So It Is!!!*

The most important message for me from this Oracle is ...

_____

_____

_____

_____

_____

_____

_____

My own personal mantra for this Oracle is ...

_____

_____

_____

_____

_____

_____

_____

Things I can do to apply this message ...

_____
_____
_____
_____
_____
_____
_____

Words of wisdom I receive from my inner voice ...

_____
_____
_____
_____
_____
_____
_____
_____

44. Boundaries

Set some boundaries. As we grow to express more and more of our True Authentic Selves, we allow ourselves to be more and more vulnerable in order to expand our consciousness and personal development. We understand that setting boundaries allows us to choose the experiences we want to be part of our life. Dramas and forces of other people's experiences no longer need to have such profound impact.

What boundaries do is define our space. We have done so much growing, we pay attention to personal raising of consciousness. We integrate spiritual practices into our lives on a daily basis. We may find some things changing up in our lives that we did not anticipate. Being open to everything that comes our way is good, realizing it is there for us to experience. At the same time it is good to make some decisions about what we want and do not want. Seriously and, of course, with love.

We may have been too willing to let others interfere with what it is we are wanting to do. We may find we cannot say "no" even when we know that is what we want (and need!) to say. We want to make this person happy even if it interferes with something else, including us and our plans! Saying "no" is a learned skill. (I read a great book years ago called *How To Say No Without Feeling Guilty* – I found it extremely helpful.)

Setting boundaries means we honor the time we need for our personal endeavors and enjoyment. We don't allow ourselves to be doormats or to be taken advantage of. We think about and start putting in place considerations about what we will and will not do. We ask ourselves questions. What makes me feel good? What does not? Then act accordingly. It is a very good exercise to take some time to think and write about this.

Remember to be kind as you set your own boundaries for yourself and others.

Let your mantra be: **I AM setting boundaries as a shield that wards off the undesirable, reflects back out the negative and encourages and keeps the love and growth I am creating in my life ... And So It Is!!!**

The most important message for me from this Oracle is ...

_____

_____

_____

_____

_____

_____

_____

My own personal mantra for this Oracle is ...

_____

_____

_____

_____

_____

_____

_____

Things I can do to apply this message ...

Words of wisdom I receive from my inner voice ...

45. Strength

Acknowledge the strength in your life! Invoking strength supports what is going on right now. Strength supports the negotiation of stress levels out there, keeping us from stretching the rubber band to the breaking point. It's about making use of all of our balancing tools and having the strength to work with what is happening in our lives to reach our personal, professional and spiritual goals.

The Universe will support you every step of the way. Deepen the processes and practices you have been working on. Confirm that now is the time to exercise mental and spiritual strength and stamina. Follow the guidance that has been coming to you. It doesn't mean you have to go all the way with what you have been receiving but it certainly does mean being strong enough and bold enough to incorporate it into your open heart. Pace yourself while you take whatever those first steps are.

If you do not feel that you have received any guidance, take a moment now to sit in contemplation. Open yourself to receive information and guidance. Do you feel a tug in any particular direction about something that needs attention? What do you want to do? What do you need to do? What do you need to focus on? Is there anything you need to change? Have the spiritual strength to take those steps.

Like building physical strength by working out, building spiritual strength is similar. The difference is spiritual strength comes from within. Building your spiritual strength activates your spirit and connection to the Divine from within. This gives you all the power you need to live a life of purpose and fulfillment, passion and joy.

We build spiritual strength with every process and practice we incorporate in our lives. See where strength needs to be. Know All Is Well.

Let your mantra be: *I AM a strong, powerful, REAL being and with that strength I activate my Spirit and Connection to the Divine ... And So It Is!!!*

The most important message for me from this Oracle is ...

_____
_____
_____
_____
_____
_____
_____

My own personal mantra for this Oracle is ...

_____
_____
_____
_____
_____
_____
_____

Things I can do to apply this message ...

_____

_____

_____

_____

_____

_____

Words of wisdom I receive from my inner voice ...

_____

_____

_____

_____

_____

_____

46. Circumspection

The path of personal and spiritual transformation is dependent upon circumspection. So, what does circumspection mean to us here, in the context of transforming our lives, accelerating our personal development? It is generally defined as *the quality of being wary and unwilling to take risks, or prudence.* Well, what is prudence? Prudence is *acting with or showing thought and care for the future.* Ah, now that fits; they go together.

There are times in our lives when we are quickly moving forward. We know that the energies are flying with us, moving us, sometimes almost effortlessly, along our path. Then there are times when things get in our way, slow us down, or seemingly bring us to a halt (although not necessarily in a bad way). Things just don't come together as easily as other times. This is when we acknowledge that it is time to be circumspect, to slow down, to check things out, to not necessarily move ahead so fast. And that's okay.

Notice these changes in the energies. Sometimes, when we are moving in a direction to which we feel completely guided, we are feeling it, knowing this is the way to go. Then we run into some difficulties or challenges. Some folks are thrown off balance and stop their forward movement. They figure it was wrong; this is not the way to go. The more consciously we view our life, the more we recognize that there are times to be circumspect.

Take time to double check what you are doing and see if it fits into the picture you hold for your reality. Understand that these pauses are there for each of us to stop and think about what we are rolling into. Make adjustments, minor or major.

As you find yourself looking at life in a new or expanded way, add to it the concept that there are times to be circumspect in what you are doing. Don't stop. Don't necessarily shift. Take a space in time. Think about being circumspect. Consider prudence. Then go forward with confidence. Let your inner guidance lead the way.

Let your mantra be: *I AM thinking carefully and touching heart space about possible risks before doing or saying anything ... And So It Is!!!*

_____

_____

_____

_____

_____

_____

_____

_____

_____

_____

The most important message for me from this Oracle is ...

_____
_____
_____
_____
_____
_____
_____

My own personal mantra for this Oracle is ...

_____
_____
_____
_____
_____
_____
_____
_____

Things I can do to apply this message ...

Words of wisdom I receive from my inner voice ...

47. Life Mastery

Life Mastery takes the view that every experience we encounter is a lesson-learning opportunity for growth. It is an expression of our True Self, an opportunity to learn or express compassion and/or unconditional love. It is a step along the path. From this perspective, life is, indeed, our teacher.

On this path of transformation, we learn and come to recognize that we are not our thoughts, minds or bodies. This is a big change from what we have been taught. We are much more. We are the energy and the consciousness behind all that. As the French philosopher and priest Pierre Teilhard de Chardin* profoundly said, *we are not human beings having a spiritual experience; we are spiritual beings having a human experience.*

Mastery is defined as *knowledge and skill that allows one to do, use or understand something as an independently recognized and certified expert or professional and having full command of a discipline or profession.* When we add the word *life* to *mastery* we see that life mastery is having the skill and command to see, and then change, the way our ego-based mind dominates our life. We recognize that we are not our thoughts. We allow the truth of Who We Are, our spiritual self, to run our life. It means we stop struggling and learn to flow. We live the experiences that come to us.

How we personally experience life mastery rests on a decision we make every day. How to be in this world, but not of it. How to be the change we want to see in the world.

Part of mastering life is paying attention to each of the experiences we have. With a Buddha-like awareness we can integrate each experience as something new, something we have not seen before, even if it has happened over and over. We see an opportunity for growth each and every time. We understand that the rifts and conflicts in life are opportunities for new seeds to be planted in places that have broken through. Life mastery is also about allowing things to be what they are, not resisting what is and staying spiritually grounded.

Let your mantra be: *I AM spiritually grounded — I walk the spiritual path with my feet on the ground and use the worldly life as a forum for personal growth ... And So It Is!!!*

The most important message for me from this Oracle is ...

_____
_____
_____
_____
_____
_____
_____

My own personal mantra for this Oracle is ...

_____
_____
_____
_____
_____
_____
_____
_____

Things I can do to apply this message ...

_____
_____
_____
_____
_____
_____
_____
_____

Words of wisdom I receive from my inner voice ...

_____
_____
_____
_____
_____
_____
_____
_____

48. Emergence

In the final steps along the path of changing our lives we find a new experience happening ... Emergence.

Emergence is defined several ways: *It is the process of coming into view, being exposed after being concealed or coming into being or becoming important or prominent.* All apply. The Oxford Dictionary says that the origin of the word emergence came from *the mid-17th century (in the sense of an 'unforeseen occurrence'): from medieval Latin emergentia, from Latin emergere, bring to light.*

Each of these concepts work for our focus here. Open to the directions we intuitively perceive as right for us and then emerge. We bring to light and expose ourselves as we do our deep inner work. We are all in the process of becoming or expressing our True Selves, as best we know, as we personally and spiritually develop. This is part of emergence.

Emergence also includes surrender and release of old aspects of our lives. We let go of old beliefs that no longer support us and old situations that have nothing to do with where we are now.

We are growing, changing and developing personally and spiritually. We can feel it; we *know* it. Many do not. Many are in chaos. Our energies support the collective. So what do we do with all this? Emerge. Now! It is the key, the energy to focus on.

Emerging ... from sleep. Emerging ... from what we used to be. Emerging ... from what we used to believe. Emerging ... to the light.

Touch the inner realms. Explore how to bring Spirit into physical reality. How to BE it. Understand that the inner universe is as infinite as the outer universe. As we allow ourselves to personally and spiritually emerge, we bring expression of our inner universe to light. We find ourselves more open with our feelings and more open with our thoughts. We are more open to being our true authentic selves and more able to live from the heart.

Let your mantra be: *I AM relinquishing the illusion of control and emerging from my cocoon into the light with eyes wide open ... And So It Is!!!*

The most important message for me from this Oracle is ...

_____

_____

_____

_____

_____

_____

_____

My own personal mantra for this Oracle is ...

_____

_____

_____

_____

_____

_____

_____

Things I can do to apply this message ...

_____
_____
_____
_____
_____
_____
_____

Words of wisdom I receive from my inner voice ...

_____
_____
_____
_____
_____
_____
_____
_____

49. Connecting at the Heart Level

Now is a time to connect ... in spirit, online or even face to face. Even social networking is a way to stay in touch. Connect with other human beings near and far.

The expression of connectedness transcends our traditional, usual ideas about connection. Connect at the heart level. Even people whose lifestyle has very limited contact with others can and do feel connected as they go about their daily lives.

Practice connectedness at the heart level by flowing love energy out through the heart as you walk your path. Escape the mind. Be present in the here and now. Have an open, friendly attitude. Smile! Look at people, trees, rocks, dirt, animals ... see all of it! Get out of the mind – look out there in the world. Many folks will respond in kind. It's about connection, about sending and receiving love.

We've all heard, *don't talk to strangers*. We have been taught that *others* are scary, so we have to be closed and unapproachable. That way no one can accost us, do us harm, talk to us, or get close to us. This fearful conditioning has been going on for a long, long time. There are certainly times when we must stay aware and alert. The more we tap into and trust our intuition, our guides and angels, the more we will feel when then things are not right. Our unseen entourage guides us when people are not to be engaged. It is about being conscious.

As we walk the path of life, connecting at the heart level with others brings joy and richness. We are, indeed, all One!

Let your mantra be: *I AM connecting at the heart level with all living beings on my journey through life ... And So It Is!!!*

The most important message for me from this Oracle is ...

_____

_____

_____

_____

_____

_____

_____

My own personal mantra for this Oracle is ...

_____

_____

_____

_____

_____

_____

_____

Things I can do to apply this message ...

_____

_____

_____

_____

_____

_____

_____

Words of wisdom I receive from my inner voice ...

_____

_____

_____

_____

_____

_____

_____

50. Confidence

Firmly and confidently ground yourself in the experience that All Is Well. With this transformation comes a release of confidence unlike any ever experienced before.

Life is a wild roller coaster ride, with ups, downs, turns, shifts, and changes on an almost daily basis. More and more issues are coming to the fore which are shaking the foundation of many lives. Changes we have never dreamed of are here in front of us. During these times it is more important than ever to pause and listen to your Spirit's prompting. No matter what your current life situation is, no matter what experience you are having, no matter what is coming at or to you, pull up and remain confident! Ground your confidence into every experience.

What is confidence? Is it a belief? Is it faith? There are qualitative differences between belief, faith and confidence. Beliefs are thoughts or opinions that are accepted as true. They are typically created from other people, or are thought patterns from the past, unless one has made the conscious effort to update them. Faith generally revolves around hope and reliance upon something without overt proof or physical evidence. Faith substantially acts on a belief and requires commitment; you can believe something without having faith in it. Both belief and faith can be questioned, or changed over the course of a lifetime.

Confidence is a feeling or awareness of your own power and relies upon one's circumstances or abilities. It is the assertion to walk your own path, to stand alone if need be, and to trust in yourself no matter what is happening.

Get and remain confident. Look inward. Let Spirit fill you. There is no wrong in your life. Be confident that you are always in the right place at the right time.

Let your mantra be: *I know the place within me where my confidence resides; I hereby release it to my Self for grounding and full expression in my life and in the world ... And So It Is!!!*

The most important message for me from this Oracle is ...

My own personal mantra for this Oracle is ...

Things I can do to apply this message ...

_____

_____

_____

_____

_____

_____

_____

_____

Words of wisdom I receive from my inner voice ...

_____

_____

_____

_____

_____

_____

_____

_____

51. Alignment

Alignment is about consciously aligning ourselves with our Source, Divine Essence, Higher Self, Soul, All That Is – however you describe that energy. Our task is to focus not only on bringing ourselves into alignment but also on maintaining the practice of staying aligned.

We humans tend to be all over the place with our energies; tossing about between the heart, the mind, the body, emotions, intellect, pleasure and what all of that creates. Shift and align those energies. Not doing so indiscriminately, but shifting into alignment with the highest good for life, family, our Planet, Solar System, Galaxy and Cosmos. Oh yes!

Following is an exercise to help align yourself when you find your feelings all over the place:

Energetically square up your shoulders. Make sure your head is straight up in the center. Pull down energy from Source into an imaginary sphere of white light just above your head, say about four feet up. Then pull up energy from your heart and wrap it around this sphere. Bring this sphere of energy down to sit on the top of your head. Allow yourself to feel this energy move through you. Feel it move down your arms, down your hips, down your legs, through the bottom of your feet into the deep crystal core of Mother Earth. Maintain this sensation. Stay with it. Be in complete alignment with Source through your physical and etheric bodies and directly into the Earth. Next, allow the energy to flow back up through you all the way back to Source and back down again as many times as you wish, ending at your heart level.

When doing this exercise, let any visions come. Write down what you see and experience. Then meditate on these visions. They can assist you in your effort to maintain alignment.

Therein lies the practice. This is the state of *walking your talk*. When we are walking our talk we are aligning daily. We constantly remind ourselves, minute by minute, to stay grounded and aligned no matter what is going on. Spiritual and personal development is the direction in which we are traveling. Now is the time to really and truly authentically align our mind, body and spirit with our Divine Essence. We are then aligned on the ethical pathway in life and to the compassion the world needs now.

Let your mantra be: *I AM aligning my Real and True Self with my Higher Self, my Spirit, my guides ... and with All That Is ... And So It Is!!!*

The most important message for me from this Oracle is ...

_____

_____

_____

_____

_____

_____

_____

My own personal mantra for this Oracle is ...

_____

_____

_____

_____

_____

_____

_____

_____

Things I can do to apply this message ...

_____

_____

_____

_____

_____

_____

_____

Words of wisdom I receive from my inner voice ...

_____

_____

_____

_____

_____

_____

_____

52. Transformation

Each and every one of us is focusing on liberating ourselves as much as possible from old ideas, old habits, old relationships and old patterns of thinking. Everything comes to an end at some point. Everything changes. It is the law of impermanence. We are experiencing the end of what could be called the *old order*. There is much change afoot!

The energy of *transformation* is just that, transforming ourselves. It is stepping more and more into becoming our best and most authentic selves. It is indeed a transformation. Inner work is required. Understand that transformation is like the shedding of a snake's old skin; we become reborn, with new skin. Shedding what is dead in our lives is a big part of transformation.

We are provided many opportunities for growth on our journey through life. Instead of lashing out or beating ourselves up when something happens that is not comfortable, stop and say, "This person or situation is my teacher!" Learn not to react. Transform from the way of the past. Embrace a new way. Do the right thing. Take the high road. Have compassion for yourself as well as others.

Massive changes are on the way. Those with hearts aligned with Spirit will be able to support the birthing of the New Reality. Allowing transformation through these changing times will keep us strong and powerful. Transform and align ego, mind and inner voice with your heart. Follow the guidance of Spirit and your Higher Knowing ... your Higher Self.

Free yourself from what is holding you back, blocking you from the next steps. Transformation is a truly worthwhile purpose and goal. The end result is the evolution of consciousness.

Let your mantra be: *I AM letting go of oppressive, restrictive, limiting attitudes and beliefs. I AM letting go of outdated ideas; I AM letting go of mental clutter. I AM cutting away to get to the core of my essence, my growth, my path, my love, my transformation ... And So It Is!!!*

The most important message for me from this Oracle is ...

_____
_____
_____
_____
_____
_____
_____

My own personal mantra for this Oracle is ...

_____
_____
_____
_____
_____
_____
_____

Things I can do to apply this message ...

_____

_____

_____

_____

_____

_____

_____

Words of wisdom I receive from my inner voice ...

_____

_____

_____

_____

_____

_____

_____

How I plan to celebrate my transformation ...

Personal Transformation Journal

Love and Trust, my dear ones ... Love and Trust!

My Transformation Journal

_____

_____

_____

_____

_____

_____

_____

_____

_____

_____

_____

_____

_____

_____

_____

~ To create the new, the old must be transformed. ~

~ The changes taking place begin within. ~

~ Fear stops transformation. ~

~ Trust whatever comes your way. ~

~ The cornerstone of our transformation is what we build to support our own personal, professional and spiritual development. ~

~ Being determined to complete goals and aspirations provides you with internal motivation and drive to accomplish whatever you need and want. ~

~ Only you know what dead branch needs to be cut away to strengthen your whole tree. ~

~ Make space for quiet time in your life. ~

~ Develop a plan to bring your visions
and dreams into reality. ~

~ Soar high above the mountains and valleys of life.
Allow yourself to see The Big Picture. ~

~ You are a unique expression of divinity. ~

~ Recognizing who you really are allows you
to shine forth in the world. ~

~ The more the true authentic self can express itself, the more love and support we invite into our lives. ~

~ Forgiveness comes through turning our attention inward
and using the spiritual energy of love. ~

~ Allow yourself to be grateful for what IS. Know in your deepest heart that all is just as it is supposed to be. ~

~ Open your heart to the Divine guidance which your non-physical team of angels and guides brings to you. ~

~ The present moment is really all there is. ~

~ Balance allows us to live a more expanded
life in these changing times. ~

~ You are here on this Earth at this time
to be a power for change. ~

~ As you learn and grow on the path of transformation
you find guidance every step of the way. ~

~ Listen to the stillness that underlies everything,
and trust your inner voice. ~

~ Expressing appreciation to others is a great way to be the change you want to see in the world. ~

~ Every day is an adventure, an opportunity
to experience something new. ~

~ Let go and flow with the natural movement
of All That Is. ~

~ Lighten up and acknowledge that at some level,
the world is a playground! ~

~ Allow yourself to express who you really are! ~

~ Kindness is needed in every dealing, every step of the way. ~

~ When we learn to laugh at ourselves, our situations,
or our lives, we lighten our souls. ~

~ Forgive yourself and love yourself unconditionally! ~

~ Allow and acknowledge
the dignity of every person you meet. ~

~ Love is the energy of healing. ~

~ Open your eyes to a new vision of All That Is. ~

~ Bring forth your own inherent wisdom. ~

~ Listen with your heart, and then take a leap of faith. ~

~ Evaluate your own self-identity.
Look within, consciously and lovingly. ~

~ Do not allow fear to stop you from abandoning
what needs to be abandoned. ~

~ Learn to be content in any and all conditions. ~

~ Use your keen powers of observation
to intuit any situation. ~

~ Our heightened perceptiveness is needed now, more than ever, to discern the truth and authenticity of what is really going on. ~

~ If we let it, change awakens us
to the sacred process that it is. ~

~ It is you, standing in the truth of Who You Are,
that knows what you want to say or do! ~

~ Your fortune lies where your passion is. ~

~ Rejoice in the feeling of Oneness with the Universe. ~

~ Step into your real True Self. Be wholly who you are. ~

~ Setting boundaries means we honor the time we need for our personal endeavors and enjoyment. ~

~ Building your spiritual strength activates
your Spirit connection to the Divine. ~

~ Let your inner guidance lead the way. ~

~ Part of mastering life is paying attention to
each of the experiences we have. ~

~ We are all in the process of becoming or expressing our True Selves. ~

~ Practice connectedness at the heart level by flowing love energy out through the heart as you walk your path. ~

~ There is no *wrong* in your life. Be confident that you are always in the right place at the right time. ~

~ When we are walking our talk we are aligning daily. ~

~ Transformation is about stepping more and more into becoming your best and most authentic self. ~

~ Free yourself from what is holding you back!
Be who you truly are! ~

ABOUT THE AUTHOR

Darity Wesley

Darity Wesley, author, lawyer, speaker, Death Diva and Modern Day Oracle experiences life to its fullest. A long time traveler on the spiritual, metaphysical, esoteric and personal development path, Darity has transformed her life many times in many ways.

Having concluded a fabulous 35 year legal career as a privacy and information security guru and business lawyer, Darity has now transitioned into focusing full time on the *Modern Day Oracle™ Wisdom Teaching Series*. Her intention for this series is to share the spiritual wisdom that she has gained along the way, including her favorite tools of transformation.

Darity has provided her *Modern Day Oracle™* messages since 2006 to subscribers all around the world. If you would like to join the *Modern Day Oracle™* community, please visit to our website and subscribe!

www.DarityWesley.com

To contact the author, please send an email to Darity@DarityWesley.com

REFERENCES

Breitman, Patti, and Hatch, Connie. *How To Say No Without Feeling Guilty.* [New York]: Random House, 2000.

Cousins, Norman. *Anatomy of an Illness: As Perceived by the Patient.* [New York]: Norton, 1979.

Dass, Ram. *Be Here Now.* 1st ed., Lama Foundation, 1971.

Tolle, Eckhart. *The Power of Now.* 1st ed., Namaste Publishing, 1997.

Wilhelm, Richard, and Cary F. Baynes. *The I Ching;* Or, *Book of Changes.* [New York]: Pantheon Books, 1950. [English text] Note: The I Ching is an ancient Chinese divination text that dates back thousands of years.

*Note: The quote cited on page 198, *We are not human beings having a spiritual experience; we are spiritual beings having a human experience* has been credited in this book to Pierre Teilhard de Chardin. And although he is the one most commonly credited for being the source of this quote, it should be noted that according to Wikiquote.org, G. I. Gurdjieff has also been given credit, and therefore the source is currently disputed.

GRATITUDE AND APPRECIATION

The creation of this book, my first in the Wisdom Teaching Series, has been a wonderful flow of love and energy with so many folks who participated and supported me in various parts of its formation. I thank each and every one for the energy and support!

To my tireless Absolutely Amazing Assistant and Graphic Designer, Paula Wansley, I give my thanks, appreciation and gratitude. Her consummate focus on facilitating the design and her perspectives on the entire work helped make *You Can Transform Your Life* an enriched dynamic tool of transformation. Her support, care and encouragement of me, personally, and of the entire process has been phenomenal. I am so very grateful for all her help.

To my Extraordinarily Excellent Editor, Melissa Morgan, who, as all good editors must, speaks her truth with aplomb, has helped me stay on the straight and narrow where necessary, time after time. Her editorial support has kept me grammatically safe and sound and you would never ever believe ellipses ... could be so involved. I am so appreciative for all she has done to support the creation of this series. She is an amazing woman.

I wish to thank David Sams for his professional creative expertise and designer's editorial eye. And to all my Fabulous Friends who provided feedback on various portions of the work, including, but not limited to, Jayne Sams, Tina Kaufman, Judie Goodin, Lindsay Nakagawa, Linda Hernandez, Wendy Mears-Kaveney, Patty Connor, Marinda Neumann, Mara Cook, Tiffany and my writing sister and forever friend, Cristina Smith. Thank you one and all.

A special thanks to my husband, Robert, who has been at my side cheering me on with all my projects, schemes and dreams. His support and love have grounded and sustained me for a lifetime, and I would not be the person I am today without it. I am so grateful for his belief in me and his love. Love really is the great transformer!

Modern Day Oracle™ Wisdom Teaching Series

You Can Transform Your Life
Go Deeper
Workbook

Darity Wesley
Melissa Morgan
Paula Wansley

You Can Transform Your Life

Go Deeper

Companion Workbook for
You Can Transform Your Life
by Darity Wesley

Provides a more in-depth exploration of the
You Can Transform Your Life process

Go Deeper contains ...

- Additional questions for each of the 52 Oracle Messages to promote deeper self-discovery and awareness.

- Bonus exercises and information to help increase intuition, spiritual strength and inner balance.

- Practical advice on how to apply *Modern Day Oracle*™ tools of transformation to all areas of your life.

For those seeking to *go deeper* on their journey of transformation

ISBN 978-0-9995425-1-4

**Winner 2017 Pinnacle Achievement Award
Games and Puzzles**

THE WORD SEARCH ORACLE

Yoga for the Brain™

Featuring Modern Day Oracle™ messages by Darity Wesley!

Every puzzle is both a challenge to be solved and a meditation for self-realization.

Filled with fascinating facts and enlightening insights.

Enjoy 60 fun-filled word search puzzles each with a hidden Oracle message!

Have fun with a purpose!

The Word Search Oracle Invites You to Play!

ISBN 978-1544211558

Made in the USA
San Bernardino, CA
06 November 2017